Argentina's

Foreign Policy, 1930-1962

Italy after Fascism, A Political History, 1943–1965. Giuseppe Mammarella.

The Volunteer Army and Allied Intervention in South Russia, 1917–1921. George A. Brinkley.

Personalities and Policies: Studies in the Formulation of British Foreign Policy in the Twentieth Century. D. C. Watt.

Peru and the United States, 1900–1962. James C. Carey.

Empire by Treaty: Britain and the Middle East in the Twentieth Century. M. A. Fitzsimons.

The USSR and the UN's Economic and Social Activities. Harold Karan Jacobson.

Chile and the United States: 1880–1962. Fredrick B. Pike.

Death in the Forest: The Katyn Forest Massacre. J. K. Zawodny.

East Central Europe and the World: Developments in the Post-Stalin Era. Stephen D. Kertesz, ed.

Soviet Policy Toward International Control of Atomic Energy. Joseph L. Nogee.

American Diplomacy in a New Era. Stephen D. Kertesz, ed.

Diplomacy in a Changing World. Stephen D. Kertesz and M. A. Fitzsimons, eds.

The Russian Revolution and Religion, 1917–1925. Edited and translated by Boleslaw Szcześniak.

Soviet Policy Toward the Baltic States, 1918–1940. Albert N. Tarulis.

INTERNATIONAL STUDIES OF THE
COMMITTEE ON INTERNATIONAL RELATIONS
UNIVERSITY OF NOTRE DAME

Introduction to Modern Politics. Ferdinand Hermens.

Freedom and Reform in Latin America. Fredrick B. Pike, ed.

What America Stands For. Stephen D. Kertesz and M. A. Fitzsimons, eds.

The Representative Republic. Ferdinand Hermens.

Theoretical Aspects of International Relations. William T. R. Fox, ed.

Catholicism, Nationalism and Democracy in Argentina. John J. Kennedy.

Christian Democracy in Western Europe, 1820–1953. Michael P. Fogarty.

Why Democracies Fail: A Critical Evaluation of the Causes for Modern Dictatorships. Norman L. Stamps.

The Fate of East Central Europe. Stephen D. Kertesz, ed.

German Protestants Face the Social Question. William O. Shanahan.

Soviet Imperialism: Its Origins and Tactics. Waldemar Gurian, ed.

The Foreign Policy of the British Labour Government, 1945–1951. M. A. Fitzsimons.

Diplomacy in a Whirlpool: Hungary between Nazi Germany and Soviet Russia. Stephen D. Kertesz.

Christian Democracy in Italy and France. Mario Einaudi and François Goguel.

Bolshevism: An Introduction to Soviet Communism. Waldemar Gurian.

Argentina's Foreign Policy, 1930-1962

By ALBERTO CONIL PAZ and
GUSTAVO FERRARI

Translated by John J. Kennedy

UNIVERSITY OF NOTRE DAME PRESS 1966
NOTRE DAME · LONDON

Originally published as
Politica exterior argentina 1930–1962
by Editorial Huemul S. A., Buenos Aires

Grateful acknowledgment is made to the Latin-American Translation Program of the Association of American University Presses for having provided the means for translation and preparation of the manuscript for this book.

Library of Congress Catalog Card Number: 66-24918
Manufactured in the United States

PREFACE

This book came out of our classes on Argentine foreign policy in Salvador University. First we and then our students discovered the lack of materials, if one disregards the pamphlet bibliography, some foreign writing—usually in exhausted editions or difficult of access—and the few Argentine works that in general employ the juridical method in order to avoid the systematic exposition of the political aspects of our international relations. The spontaneous enthusiasm of the editors did the rest.

The result is a manual, according to the designation of the series in which it is published. It is a draft, an outline, fatally imperfect in initiatives of greater extent. This characteristic explains why we have preferred to omit footnotes and to place a detailed bibliography at the end of the book.

Finally, we wish to thank those who have helped in many indispensable ways the preparation and publication of this book —especially the personnel of the Archives of the Ministry of Foreign Affairs and Worship, whose cordial assistance always supplemented the scarcity of the technical means.

A.C.P.
G.F.

TRANSLATOR'S NOTE

The importance of the study by Dr. Conil Paz and Dr. Ferrari is that it presents an Argentine assessment of the conduct of foreign relations during three critical decades in modern Argentine history. Respect for this fact has guided the work of translation and has placed an obligation on the translator to render accurately and faithfully in English the thought and spirit of the authors and to exclude anything of the translator's value judgment from the text.

Even scrupulous observance of this obligation, however, has not of itself eliminated all problems of translation. Those that should be noted here chiefly concern the task of putting back into English the authors' Spanish-language citations of English-language documents. In a few cases it has been necessary for the sake of clarity to extend slightly the quotations beyond what the authors presented in Spanish. In two or three other instances the authors have apparently had access to Spanish-language citations of English-language sources that are not available, or at any rate not yet available, to the public in the United States. In the latter cases I have sought to indicate in the footnotes how this material has been handled in translation.

CONTENTS

1: THE CONSEQUENCES OF THE CRISIS

THE WORLD CRISIS, 1929

After 1929 the economic crisis held the entire world in its embrace of privation; no country escaped the consequences. The crash of the New York Stock Exchange extended rapidly to all the exchanges of the world, abruptly put an end to the flow of American loans to Europe, and thus provoked a great urgency to recover money invested in the less safe countries. The logical consequence was that the short-term foreign credits were frozen in view of the impossibility on the part of the states to maintain their payments. At the same time the creditor countries were weakened financially by the immobility of their investments, while the debtor countries could not obtain loans with which to resolve their most pressing necessities.

The crisis passed from country to country. The wave of the depression extended first, and with the sharpest effects, to the countries whose economic structure was particularly fragile. At the end of 1929 Uruguay and Argentina suspended payments in gold, and Canada submitted the gold standard to certain restrictions. In 1930 Brazil, Chile, Australia, New Zealand, Venezuela, and Mexico suffered monetary depreciations ranging between 9 and 50 per cent. The center of minimum resistance, Austria gave way in May 1931 to the pressure that paralyzed all business. The deafening collapse of the Creditanstalt in Vienna—the strongest banking institution of Central Europe—brought down a whole system of financial obligations. In July Germany ordered a bank holiday, a moratorium, and imposed exchange control. In order to conserve parity with gold for their respective currencies, the majority of Central European countries adopted exchange control so as to avoid exportation of funds. Consequently, France was jolted in its turn. The true financial hurricane fell upon England, who freed herself of the obligation to sell gold, abandoning thus the gold standard—a measure copied immediately by a score of European and American countries.

A vertical fall of prices followed immediately after the financial crisis. Between 1929 and 1932 goods in general lost more than one-third of their value, and raw materials lost more than half, reaching the point in 1933 when prices failed to recover even production costs. Exhausted treasuries and deficits without precedent were common. The majority of the countries suspended payments; insolvency became general; investments were reduced to the minimum; and hoarding became the order of the day. Everything was plunging in the realm of public as well as private finance.

Crisis fed on crisis: paralyzation of industry, closing of factories, downturn of business, vertical fall of rents, and increasing unemployment. In 1932, low point in the crisis, there existed in the world—excluding Asia and Africa—more than 30 million unemployed.

All this accentuated even more the division between the economic units that had existed before the war. By means of protectionist practices of economic nationalism states sought to save their economies, making difficult thereby commercial interchange and providing for themselves all of their material necessities. Economic nationalism, policies of autarky, and agrarian protectionism gradually spelled out the elimination of international exchange in order to achieve economic autonomy. Thus was sought the strengthening of national economies, so as to prop up the power of each nation.

This general policy introduced into international economic relations certain novelties that took the form of import quotas, subsidies, increase of tariffs, and exchange control. The various countries raised impassable barriers that impeded mutual understanding and economic interchange. Hence the spectacle of an excess of production and goods in some nations, while in others want without measure: on the one side overproduction, and on the other side difficulty in acquiring the basic necessities; or abundance vs. crisis and misery.

With the progress of protectionist tendencies, which tended toward autarky, the industrial countries of Europe—the chief markets for exportable agricultural and pastoral surpluses—aspired to independence through their own food production. Germany, France, and Italy developed their agriculture because of a strong protectionism. England also threw herself into this practice after 1931 under Minister of Agriculture Walter Elliot. The objective was the reagriculturalization of Europe.

France was the first European country to establish import quotas. For determined agricultural and pastoral products she instituted quantitative limitations and distributed them according to countries, giving a proportionate quantity to each one. In addition to the tariffs, France created a surtax according to exchange differentials, thereby placing major obstacles in the way of commercial transactions. Meat quotas were distributed in accordance with the importations from each country; Argentina was granted an insignificant share.

Germany followed the same policy of prohibitive and changeable tariffs with regard to imports. Germany almost closed her market by reinstating a law of sanitary inspection from 1902 that prohibited the importation of beef carcasses from which the viscera had been removed. The quota of 50,000 frozen beef imported from Argentina was abolished. Italy followed the same path, aggravated by her policy of raising production when it set off the famous "battle of the wheat."

The United States, in order to save her economy, put new obstacles in the way of interchange and passed the Smoot-Hawley law in June 1930. This greatly harmful law raised customs duties up to 50 per cent of the assessed value of the goods. It had been proposed to re-establish in favor of agriculture the balance of factors as they existed before the crisis, with the object of protecting the agricultural interests of the West.

England, on her part feeling the pressure of the autarky policies followed by the great powers and trying to be self-sufficient, resolved to convoke in 1932 an imperial economic conference where the principle of "imperial preference" would be formulated. In reality, as early as 1931 and with the same objective, there had been promulgated the Abnormal Importations Customs Duties Act, to be in effect for six months. In this the government was authorized to establish protective tariffs up to 100 per cent *ad valorem* on all the goods entering the United Kingdom (with some exceptions), but imperial products were exempt from this tax. The Wheat Act burdened with difficulties the importation of foreign grain, in order to protect the national producers who were at a disadvantage on account of a cost of production higher than the respective price of the world market.

THE IMPERIAL CONFERENCE OF OTTAWA, 1932

The Ottawa conference then met in circumstances of world economic crisis, of a protectionist policy toward foreign goods, and a preferential policy respecting those of the Empire. Twelve agreements were signed embracing the following fundamental points: Great Britain obligated herself (1) to maintain the preference of 10 per cent of the law of 1932, an advantage which she could not modify without consulting the dominions, and (2) to establish duties on foreign products and establish quotas on the same products.

On their part the dominions obligated themselves (1) to maintain and establish certain preferences; (2) to protect against the competition of the products of the metropolis only those industries that might have serious possibilities of survival; and (3) not to surpass in their protective tariffs a level that would permit the manufactures of Great Britain a reasonable competition with local products.

The purpose sought with this "imperial preference" was to achieve an increased interchange between the United Kingdom and the dominions, so as to maintain the stability of prices and to establish restrictions on importations from countries that did not form part of the Commonwealth. In the debates at the Ottawa conference there was talk of Argentine competition with respect to products of the dominions. Bruce, the representative of Australia, as well as Canada's representative, Bennet, referred to the necessity of protection for their meat and wheat against the Argentine. South Africa alleged a capacity for the development of large herds, but for this is needed preferences in advance since the Argentine was flooding the English markets and making impossible, under these conditions, the development of South Africa's trade.

In the agreement celebrated by the United Kingdom with Australia and New Zealand it was extablished that the British government would progressively dislodge from England the foreign competitors, so as to broaden the range of supply from the products of the dominions.

As a consequence of the Ottawa conference the United Kingdom limited the importation of chilled beef and frozen mutton, taking as a base the total quantities imported between July 1, 1931, and June 30, 1932. The foreign importations of beef and frozen mutton for the same year were reduced quarterly to the following percentages: first quarter, 90 per cent; second quarter, 85 per cent; third quarter, 80 per cent; fourth quarter, 65 per cent. Frozen mutton and beef were logically the ones that suffered with greatest intensity from these reductions; mutton dropped from 69,000 tons to 57,000 in 1933, and beef from 10,000 to 8,700. As to chilled beef, earlier in August 1932 the

English import quota had been reduced by 10 per cent, indicating thereby for the year 1933 a reduction of around 100,000 tons—thus, in the year of the Ottawa conference, the drop from 390,000 tons to 290,000.

THE STATISM OF THE CONSERVATIVES

Our economy, with its foundations in the exportation of farm products, was gravely exposed in the economic readjustment of the European markets. Two factors placed the country in a situation that needed to be faced and resolved. These were protectionism with its customs barriers and the movement of "return to the soil," which were in keeping with the ideals of autarky then in vogue. The problem was even more grave with respect to our stores of chilled beef because we were then exporting to Great Britain almost 99 per cent of the same.

The Justo government decided with its "new commercial policy" to clear up the difficulties and uncertainties in our traditional markets by means of a determined governmental intervention that would regulate the process of our foreign commerce within a world system of directed economy. Thus in our country began the practice of bilateralism. Traditional free trade, supported by the most favored-nation clause, was replaced by bilateral conventions on the basis of preferential clauses. It should not be forgotten, however, that especially at the farm products level the statist antecedents are more remote: one can cite, for example, the initiatives of Deputy Sánchez Sorondo between 1922 and 1933; also the book published by the Sociedad Rural Argentina in 1927, whose title already postulated the "necessity of the intervention of the state."

This interference from the state in our international trade, manifest for the first time in the Roca-Runciman Agreement, arose entirely from a plan for the regulation of production in accordance with demand, which at that time was reaching its lowest point because of the lack of acquisitive capacity of the consumer. Regulation was also manifest through a system of controls that permitted the maintenance of a stable value of production within the domestic market. It was the epoch during which were established regulating boards for the purpose of regulating and controlling production, the epoch that created the Central Bank and the *Instituto Movilizador de Inversiones Bancarias* (institute to mobilize bank investments). The agreement with the United Kingdom completed this picture of state interventionism characteristic of the Conservative governments after 1932 and marked the abandonment of the traditional free trade that had characterized the era of the great Argentine prosperity.

THE ROCA-RUNCIMAN AGREEMENT

The Roca-Runciman Agreement had as its fundamental objective the obtaining of normal quotas for our exports in addition to that already noted of regulating our foreign commerce. It also sought to establish an automatic system whereby foreign exchange arising from the export of Argentine products to the United Kingdom would be used for the payment of imports from England and for the income accruing to the great capital investments in our country.

But its political note, and therefore its most important, was to be found in the determination to thus make complementary the agricultural economy of Argentina with the industrialized economy of England.

For three months an Argentine delegation undertook to deal with the Board of Trade and with British Minister of Commerce Walter Runciman. The Argentine delegation was headed by Vice-President Julio A. Roca, Jr., and included Miguel Angel Cárcano, Raúl Prebisch, Carlos Brebbia, Guillermo Leguizamón, and Aníbal Fernández Beiró. The negotiations sought to reconcile the vital interests of both parties: for the Argentines meat; for the English the exchanges.

Nevertheless, as it was denounced in the Chamber of Deputies on occasion of the ratification of the agreement, the question of the exchanges did not figure in the matters that the Argentine mission carried in its portfolio. In effect only Minister of Agriculture Antonio de Tomaso appeared to have noted the minimum requirements that Roca ought to sustain in London without alluding to the exchange rate. His statement in a note of January 5, 1933, directed to Foreign Minister Saavedra Lamas, stated:

1. That we be permitted to introduce into Great Britain a minimum of 390,445 tons of chilled beef, 57,772 tons of frozen mutton (1933), 8,855 tons of frozen beef (1933), any quality of pork products, any quantity of frozen pork, any quantity of preserved meat, and that during the time in which the Ottawa agreements are in force these quantities cannot be reduced or burdened with duties of any kind.

2. Whenever Clause 8 of the agreement with Australia is applied, preference will be given to Argentina.

3. There will be no increase in the 10 per cent *ad valorem* duty on the following products of Argentine origin . . . nor will quantities of imports be restricted: hides, tallow, preserved meat, casein, extract and essence of meat, sausage stuffing, dressed domestic poultry, barley, wheat flour, peanuts, linseed oil, and so forth.

4. Products currently appearing on the free list (such as maize) will continue with this character and shall not be the object of restrictions with regard to quantity.

5. Duties on wheat, lard, cheese, fruits, and dairy products . . . cannot be increased in the future for Argentina, or the importation restricted.

. . . because of its importance there ought to be separate consideration of the demand regarding the fixing of a specific quota for Argentina and the intervention of the Argentine government in its distribution.

. . . therefore, this Ministry considers that the claim relative to the assignment of a quota to the Argentine Republic
ought to be a claim of first importance, if not the capital
claim . . . public opinion will not comprehend, if in respect
to this claim we do not obtain full satisfaction. The British
government cannot fear anything from it or from its approval.

The Argentine delegation had without any doubt a strong
base for negotiations. This lay in the serious problem that was
represented for the British in the extensive frozen sums accruing
from the income on their investments in Argentina. Under the
exchange system obtaining in the country since 1931, this income could not be remitted to the United Kingdom. This
blocked exchange of remittances payable to British creditors up
to about 150 million pesos at the time of the convention.

For Great Britain it was essential to mobilize the blocked
funds, as well as to obtain a guarantee that once mobilization
had been arranged they would not again be blocked by the
Argentine Exchange Commission. In turn, for Argentina it was
necessary, at least while the Ottawa agreements were in force,
to stabilize a position in the British market of chilled meats.
What Argentina could achieve in Great Britain with meat
depended on what it would yield in exchange, or vice versa.

At the very beginning of the discussions with British authorities John Simon and Walter Runciman confirmed to Dr. Roca
that the solution to the problem of the exchanges "was the
essential condition for the success of the negotiations." In these
circumstances the chief of the mission sent a cable to Foreign
Minister Saavedra Lamas in which he informed him that:

The British Government has subordinated all its policy in
the course of the negotiations to the arrangement of the
blocked money and to the availability of exchange. It has
been proposed not only to guarantee the possibilities of British export business but also to guarantee the payment of the
revenue from the extensive capital investments.

"I cannot assure," he said to me, "the success of a policy

that guarantees to the Argentine Republic the introduction
of her products within the possibilities created by the Ottawa
agreements if you people do not give me a solid base of support which British opinion will recognize only in the solution
of the problems of exchange. With this base I dare to pledge
myself to come out successful over the strong opposition that
I shall encounter in Parliament against all such arrangements.
Without them I am convinced beforehand that I cannot even
present the question."

 . . . if these arrangements are not carried out, it is not impossible to think that Great Britain (not in reprisal but in defense
of her own capital and her own domestic business) could consider the adoption of measures tending to regulate exchange
and blocking pounds sterling that may accrue from the sale of
Argentine products for the purpose of utilizing them in payment of importations and revenues. Such hypothesis reflects
the suggestions made by some influential man of the City.

For "the three enervating months" of negotiation the possible
base of agreement turned on the problem of the exchanges;
Argentina agreed to concede up to 25 per cent of available
exchange. For its part London was not interested in a partial
solution but instead sought a total solution of the problem, since
the immobilized capital represented 33 per cent of available
exchange.

Finally, on May 2, 1933, the negotiators signed the "Accessory Convention to the Treaty of Peace and Friendship of 1825,
in order to increase and facilitate commercial interchange between the Argentine Republic and the United Kingdom of
Great Britain and Ireland." The treaty included three texts or
three different agreements: the chief text, made up of six long
chapters—which for better comprehension were divided into
paragraphs—or the convention properly so called; an additional
explanatory protocol composed of ten declarations; and a customs convention stipulating in ten articles the tariff reductions

conceded in compensation to Great Britain, minutely detailed, which was later worked out in Buenos Aires on December 26, 1933. The principal points of the convention were:

1. *Meats.* The United Kingdom by reason of the importance of the chilled beef industry for Argentina guaranteed an import quota not less than the quantities exported by Argentina to said country between July 1931 and June 1932, which reached the total of 390,000 tons. This assured import quota could be restricted only to guarantee the remunerative level of prices within the market of the United Kingdom. But in order that this restriction might be put into effect, it would be necessary to consult in advance and to exchange information with the Argentine government.

It was also provided that the United Kingdom could reduce by 10 per cent the quota of chilled beef guaranteed by the convention if "due to unforeseen circumstances" the government of the United Kingdom considered it necessary, but for this it was necessary to consult the Argentine government and the governments of the other exporting countries including those of the Commonwealth, so as to agree upon the reduction of their importations of chilled and frozen beef (Article 1, first part of second paragraph). In the case of a reduction greater than 10 per cent Great Britain was obliged to reduce in equal proportion the importations of chilled or frozen beef coming from the countries of the Commonwealth. For frozen beef and mutton progressive percentages of reduction were established; these ranged from an initial 10 per cent up to 35 per cent at the time the convention would go out of effect.

2. *Exchanges.* As long as a system of exchange control should exist in the Argentine Republic, the total sum of exchange in pounds sterling arising from the sale of Argentine products in England would be used to satisfy the remittance claims from Argentina to the United Kingdom (Article 1, first paragraph). An exception was made allowing for a prior reasonable deduc-

tion, in order to maintain service on the Argentine public foreign debt in countries other than the United Kingdom. Thus with the earnings of Argentine exports to England there was a guarantee of the payment of goods exported by the English and the payment of dividends to bond and share holders. In return for the British guarantee assuring the exportation of meats similar to that of the years prior to Ottawa, Argentina conceded to the British a proportion of exchange equal to the sum of earnings from Argentine exports. Utilizing the very words of Lisandro de la Torre who regarded this provision as just, England would be the owner of the exchange she produced, with allowance of a deduction of that portion reserved for the service of the foreign debt in other countries.

The balances still remaining unpaid for want of exchange in pounds sterling would be paid by means of bonds in that currency provided by a loan which the Argentine government contracted at par value for twenty years and with an interest of 4 per cent annually. In reality it was more a matter of a credit than of a loan, for in this manner debts were balanced in pounds without the necessity of having the corresponding sums leave Buenos Aires. Although the conditions of the loan were beneficial for Argentina, the parliamentary debate revealed that the United Kingdom was obtaining on the other side of the ledger tariff reductions of about 12 million pesos annually, which raised the real interest by about 10 per cent additional.

3. *Tariffs.* Both countries conceded advantages in tariff materials. As the Roca mission had no powers in this respect, it was established in Article 3 that as soon as possible there would be a complementary agreement relative to tariffs and quantitative regulations applied to the products of both countries. The tariff convention, which was its result, authorized the freeing of coal, coke, and British fuel; for their part the British would not apply new duties or taxes to "meat, bacon, hams, wheat, flax, corn, and extract of quebracho imported from the Argentine." An-

nexes 1 and 2 of the tariff convention offered a list of British articles favored by reduction and consolidation of duties. Annexes 3 and 4 formulated reciprocally the list of Argentine products benefited by free entry into the English market, consolidated taxes and the nonimposition of quantitative limitations, except for those already established for meat and their derivatives.

4. *Import licenses.* Within the total quota guaranteed by the English government there was established a system of import licenses, which that government authorized and controlled. In turn, if "the Argentine government or the Argentine stock men under a special law had the possession, control and administration of enterprises that did not pursue primarily the ends of private gain, but merely a better regulation of business for the purpose of assuring reasonable benefits to the stock men," then the government of the United Kingdom recognized a free quota for such enterprises up to a maximum of 15 per cent of the total amount of the importation (Article 3 of the protocol). For this the English government obligated itself to report periodically the permits that it had authorized in connection with the importation of meat from Argentina. With respect to the import quota, that is, the 85 per cent remaining, its management and distribution remained in the hands of the North American and English meat packing plants, which controlled entirely the meat business of the country.

As will be seen later on, this point was the subject of very lively discussion when the convention came up for ratification in Congress. It was argued that the disposition "legalized the committee on freight," and that it entailed a diminution of Argentine sovereignty in that it disregarded an irrenouncible right of our government, namely, that of controlling its own foreign commerce. In reality the Argentine delegates had, in the meeting of the subcommittee on meats, stated as a matter of principle the necessity of having their own government assign the quota in order to realize their purpose of giving to the Ar-

gentine stock men an increasing direct intervention. The discontent of the producers arose from the fact that while they
were not obtaining remunerative prices for their animals, the
meat packing enterprises were making great profits. On that
occasion Cárcano maintained that public opinion would not be
satisfied if the negotiations did not give the intervention to the
Argentine government in the measure necessary to carry out its
purposes of defending the cattle business.

To this the British delegation was opposed, the spokesman
being H. F. Carlill, who said that such a measure would give
his government serious concern on the following points: the difficulty of harmonizing this procedure with the necessity of regulating the market suitably; the fear that there might thus be set
loose a disorderly competition between the present companies
and any new ones; and the possibility that the interest of the
British companies might be attacked. The English futhermore
were quite upset by the lack of exact studies on the meat business, since the absence of a thorough estimate would detract
from the seriousness of any corrective measure that might be
undertaken. To correct this absence they proposed the creation
of an impartial investigating commission that would inquire
deeply into the conduct of the great meat packing businesses.
They also promised that, if the investigation showed the charges
against the companies to be justified, then indeed they would
be disposed to collaborate with the Argentine government in
order to compel them (the companies) to abide by equitable
norms. They would be willing to carry action to the point of
withdrawing import licenses from the delinquent meat packing
firms. An overeagerness for exactitude prevailed in the Argentine
delegation over a matter that should have been simply a political
attitude. True enough, the country at the time had neither
legal instruments nor meat packing industries sufficiently developed to warrant the adoption of a more rigid attitude on this
point. The English delegation recognized Argentine control on

the export quota only to the extent of 13 per cent. The English maintained it would be difficult to persuade the House of Commons that it was just to deflect a greater percentage from the present channels of business, especially since the Argentine government lacked the necessary experience with equipment. Roca requested 20 per cent as a minimum. After much discussion 15 per cent was yielded to the Argentine government, and it was established that both countries would collaborate in a joint investigation of the meat business.

5. *Benevolent treatment of British capital.* In the sphere of its constitutional attributions the Argentine government obligated itself to accord a benevolent treatment to the undertakings of British capital.

6. *Investigation of the meat business.* Both governments would collaborate in a joint investigation of the economic and financial structure of the meat business in order to assure a reasonable benefit to the stock men. In 1938, the convention having lapsed, the Anglo-Argentine combined committee for the investigation of the meat business published its conclusions, which were limited to the juridical order of each country.

7. *Sausage stuffings.* A rationalization of the importation of stuffings was established for the British market, so that there might be no excess over the normal proportion to other meats imported from the Argentine.

8. *Duration.* The time was fixed at three years.

PARLIAMENTARY DEBATE

The examination of the treaty began in the Chamber of Deputies on July 18, 1933, with a defense of the position of the government offered by Deputy Adrián C. Escobar.

The most vigorous criticism came from the Socialist deputy, Nicolás Repetto, who, rising above the immediate circumstances, went back to the general principles of political economy which in his judgment ought to guide the foreign conduct of Argentina. With clarity he pointed out the statist features of the treaty and the risks for the future of the country. He censured bilateral agreements as characteristic of abusive intervention of the state in the economy and as contrary to the free trade tradition on which Argentine progress had been founded:

> . . . what is fundamental for a country like ours is to keep wide-open doors and at the same time to require open doors of the rest of the world. By treaties such as the one under discussion, governments take in charge functions that in our judgment ought to remain free. It may appear extraordinary for a Socialist to say this, but in reality it is necessary to shout it in view of the extraordinary and inconceivable extravagances that we witness in this order of commercial policy placed under the aegis of the governments. The direct dealing between the elements most interested in business matters in each country is now impossible. The governments interpose themselves . . . there will be no possibility that the producers of Argentine cattle concern themselves directly with the English consumer. It will be necessary that they pass forcibly through the crushing gallows established by a triumphant officialism.

After maintaining that the Ottawa conference was a violation of the Anglo-Argentine treaty of 1825, he specified other criticisms concerning the new agreement, especially the freeing of the English funds that had been accumulating in Argentina, because this preference would arouse jealousy in the other countries (as indeed it did occur with the United States). He also objected to the provision that reduced to 15 per cent the export quota permitted to national enterprise, under the system of import licenses, because he considered that the clause of the treaty which thus established it had limited the freedom of the Republic to regulate the exportation of her own products.

Deputy Julio A. Noble followed him in the analysis of the

THE CONSEQUENCES OF THE CRISIS

convention. He emphasized the inferior situation for negotiation in which Argentina found herself for lack of a meat law when the delegation went to London—"to England," he said, "whose hands were tied by the Ottawa agreements we could have opposed, also a situation created by a law of Congress." But his principal objection was in his criticism of the system of licenses established by the convention in favor of England, which already implied a discredit to Argentine sovereignty, in disregarding an irrenouncible right of our government—that of controlling its foreign commerce. It signified an official recognition of the meat trust that was regulating its commerce; and it made more difficult, if not impossible, the defense of the Argentine cattle industry. He maintained that it was impossible to "accept the intervention of the British government in the exchange control and to resign oneself to renouncing the fiscalization of exports by imposition of the same government"; that "the London government recognizes in the dominions the right of administering the quota; that it recognizes it also in the government of Denmark and only disregards the right in the government of Argentina." Regarding the exchanges, he argued that the loan of 120 million pesos at 4 per cent interest and without amortization for five years had been achieved by means of a harmful manipulation of the exchanges. "The minister of finance was in reality the only one who could feel victorious with the signing of the treaty. Nevertheless, the list of exemptions presented by the English government amounted to more than 12 million pesos. That is to say, for the sum of the loan we shall pay not only 4 per cent interest but 12 million pesos additionally."

In the Senate Lisandro de la Torre analyzed the treaty. He opposed the practice of preferential bilateralism imposed by the treaty itself. Like Noble he paused to attack harshly the regime of export licenses for meats.

It is a very grave error that the executive has committed

in accepting in the convention the establishment and legaliza-
tion of the domination of the freight conference organized
by the meat packers in order to distribute and monopolize the
export of Argentine meat. Nothing else can be signified by
placing unconditionally 85 per cent of the Argentine quota in
hands of the British government so that the latter may pass
it on to the packers, with our government denying that in the
Argentine Republic packing enterprises can function when
they propose to seek ends of particular benefit. With this
there is a general renunciation of the defense of the Argentine
cattle business.

Continuing the line of argument that the abandonment of
control of exportation of Argentine meat was the equivalent of
the abandonment of national interest, he maintained that the
convention established the possibility of foreign packers pursu-
ing ends of commercial utility, while Argentine packers were
prohibited from putting themselves in the same situation. He
closed his speech with a proposition containing in brief the
entire thesis of anti-imperialism in Argentine international policy:
"Don't come to us with conventions that place vital factors of
the Argentine cattle industry under the supervision of a foreign
nation."

For his part Senator José Nicolás Matienzo in taking the
North American example from the law of 1930, which authorized the President to increase tariffs on products from those
countries that harmed trade with the United States, said that
Argentina in view of the discriminatory treatment in the Ottawa
agreements ought to have increased by 50 per cent the duties
on English textiles and metal articles. The criticism of Matienzo
put aside any ideological question and went directly to the
political level and more concretely to the form in which the
convention had been negotiated:

> What I regret is that there has been no attempt in this
> business to exploit a little more the circumstance that there
> are in Argentina 600 million pounds . . . these 600 million

pounds are safe in our country. No reprisal of any sort has been taken against them. On the contrary, everyone recognizes that the railroads owned by English shareholders continue with their high tariffs and continue concealing their capital.

A PRECEDENT

Both in the practice of bilateralism and in the political decision to make the Argentine economy complementary to the English the Roca-Runciman convention had an immediate precedent in the agreement, subscribed November 8, 1929, between the English mission headed by Viscount Vincent D'Abernon and the government of Yrigoyen. This was also the first attempt to place international commercial transactions under the direction of the state instead of in the private channels as had been done up to this moment.

Through this agreement reciprocal credits between Great Britain and Argentina were established to the value of 100 million pesos. The United Kingdom with this credit acquired cereals and other products; with its credit Argentina acquired, through bidding or through direct purchase, rolling stock for the state railways.

When the agreement was sent to Congress for ratification, the Socialist deputies opposed it. Enrique Dickmann maintained that through this agreement the United Kingdom would not buy more than it was buying up to that time. According to his judgment no new market had been won for Argentine grains, because England was accustomed to buy much more than 100 million pesos' worth of grain each year. On the other hand, Argentina obligated herself to buy noncustomary products that were not offered at bargain prices. Dickmann alleged that the prices of English rolling stock were very high, and that Great Britain never had obtained a bid from among the many undertaken by the state railways. The reason lay in the high prices of British products as compared with those offered by Germany, United States, and Belgium. He also attacked the convention on the grounds that it constituted a concealed authorization for the state railways to dispose of 100 million pesos in buying materials without the previous requirement of competitive bidding, since Article 6 authorized direct purchase.

Federico Pinedo, at that time an independent Socialist deputy, also attacked the treaty. "This convention is a compromise for us," he said, "and it accords absolute liberty to Great Britain." He repeated Dickmann's argument maintaining that Argentina was opening a credit whereby customarily purchased products would continue to be bought and that by contrast Argentina was obligating herself to acquire in the United Kingdom products which could be bought anywhere, and more cheaply. Going into the nature of the convention he educed that it was not bilateral, "but only a unilateral Argentine obligation." Regarding the fact that Anglo-Argentine interchange was always favorable to our country, he added that "Practically, this obliges us to buy in a certain form in order to balance the credit and in a market that could be very expensive, while the English will buy here as in the world market at current prices." Antonio de Tomaso added that "This is not the beginning of any new commercial policy, for it is possible to expect the same product buyers for our market as before, when backed by the English government. This is simply a loan, a new loan of 100 million pesos made by the Bank of the Nation. The Bank may invest it without the control of anybody at its will in the acquisition of rolling stock. . . ." Although the agreement was approved by the Deputies, the Senate, on the contrary, rejected it.

IDEOLOGICAL ECHOES: THE THEME OF IMPERIALISM

In 1934 Rodolfo and Julio Irazusta had published *La Argentina y el imperialismo británico*. It presented an approach, which

whether accepted or not, was at least original. The thesis of
the book is that granted the fidelity to foreign interests—in this
case British on the part of government members (a continuation
of the *unitarios*, holders of public power since Caseros)—it was
impossible to expect any diplomatic success from the activity of
Vice President Roca in London. The Irazusta brothers, together
with other young men who were grouped around the journal
Nueva República, fought behind the figure of General Uriburu
for an institutional and political renovation of the country. The
triumph of the faction of President Justo in the army and in
the elections of 1932 made it impossible for the ideals to be
realized and, therefore, the Roca-Runciman Treaty found them
in opposition.

The first part of the book deals with the negotiation of the
treaty from which arose the statement of Guillermo Leguizamón, "Argentina resembles an important British dominion," and
the statement of Roca, chief of the mission, "Thus a writer
of jealous personality has been able to say that Argentina, on
account of its reciprocal interdependence, is from the economic
point of view an integral part of the British Empire." These
phrases, without exception, will be repeated in all the anti-
imperialist literature that approaches this theme.

The authors maintain that affairs of state should not be
teamed with commercial matters, since the latter must be submitted to the policy of the nation and to the permanent interests of the people, which many times run counter to those of
their trade. They imputed this error to the governing clique,
which considered the country strictly from the aspect of market
and disregarded the Argentine interests that might differ from
the interests of the foreign commerce established in the country
—and even from the national production itself. Therefore, the
lack of a policy had carried the Roca mission to the point of
considering commercial interests of Argentina as the fundamental thing, and of not trying on the political level a move
that would permit political interests of the nation to dominate.

They criticized the position of political inferiority in which the Argentine negotiators had placed themselves spontaneously by going to London. The threat of the Ottawa agreements should have been resisted with reverse threats of protectionism and economic nationalism.

Before undertaking the negotiations the way we had before, it was preferable to stay home, to take reprisals, as the Ottawa conference was provoking us to take them and to wait. Perhaps not much time might have passed before they would have invited us to negotiate.

Beforehand, a series of measures should have been taken: lowering of the railroad freight rates, together with customs protection of petroleum; the announcement of a possible official in-preparation monopoly of exportable meat; and a decided protectionism for Argentine manufacturers, which "could have perhaps furnished magic effects," that is, a detailed and complex reform of the state.

The book closes with a historical analysis. The *unitario* restoration in 1932, under which the "nation knelt before the foreigner abdicating its sovereignty," was, according to the authors, the principal reason why the Roca negotiation would inevitably result in ruin and, consequently, in a convention so politically inopportune.

The Irazustas' book is the first coherent formulation of the myth of British imperialism among us, but without incurring the economic monism from which their Marxist followers would not succeed in escaping. For the latter, the Roca-Runciman convention would be the proof that justified the acclimatization of Argentina to the pseudo-scientific simplifications of the Leninist theory of imperialism. A long series of important works (Rodolfo Puiggrós, José V. Liceaga, Raúl Scalabrini Ortiz, Luis V. Sommi, and Ricardo M. Ortiz) would maintain that part of the national increment was crossing the ocean and was going to London. Great Britain gobbled, like a barrel without a bottom, the agricultural and pastoral production of Argentina and, in spite of it, the country remained always a debtor. As a cause of this economic dependence, the relations between Argentina and England developed on a plane of subordination of the former government to the imperialist objectives of the latter government.

Such literature created a kind of political metaphysics by means of which everything has an interpretation accessible from the angle of imperialism. This error, product of the absence of a strictly political approach to the problem that Anglo-Argentine relations pose, leads those who uphold the anti-imperialist thesis to believe in the infallibility of the empire. This inhuman quality of the adversary definitely places the Argentines in a position of notable disadvantage with respect to the English, for it holds the former to be weak humans and the latter to be "geniuses of a profane paradise."

The hesitation of the Argentines in the face of the challenge to possess their own country would be doomed, if not to ineluctable economic laws, then to the subterranean and persevering intelligence of the British. From this forced point of view imperialism becomes an omnipotent and omniscient monster, provided with a thousand eyes and a thousand arms, which never fails to foresee and is never mistaken, and from whose malign ways nothing or no one can escape. Apart from being false and discouraging, such interpretation is nothing more than a timid attempt to cover, with a pious veil, the Argentine incompetence to resolve their most important problems. Such an approach can denote only the "transference of faults," or the alienation of national problems and possibilities.

Nevertheless, the positive aspect of the theme and its force in Argentine politics should not be underestimated.

2: BETWEEN EUROPE AND AMERICA

BEFORE JUSTO

At the beginning of this century's third decade, the two most influential countries of America—the United States and Argentina—professed a curious and symmetrical isolationism.

In the United States such constant temptation was represented by the Republican administration. Woodrow Wilson's universalist vocation did not succeed in imposing itself on the Senate of his country; nor had the latter entered the League of Nations created by the initiative of that visionary President. With respect to America, the attenuation of the policy of the big stick had not reached the point of a positive formula.

The diplomacy of Yrigoyen also was characterized by its isolationism and by its passivity. After a recalcitrant neutrality, in spite of the offenses suffered—and in spite of the opinion of the man in the street as well as the opinion of Congress—Argentina withdrew from the League of Nations in 1920. She had failed in her attempt to seat herself along with the victors in the peace conference and to propose amending the pact by allowing the conquered countries to be immediately included.

The American version of this policy was no better. For Honorio Pueyrredon preached in the desert in the Sixth Inter-American Conference of Havana in 1928 when he failed with his attempt to lower customs barriers and to impose a project of nonintervention. As a consequence of these reverses, Argentina did not attend the International Conference of American States on Conciliation and Arbitration held in Washington in 1928 and 1929. The attitude of that period was the fruit of a policy of retreat, which embraced the entire international scene; withdrawal from the League had brought about either an abandonment or a disregarding of international relations.

After 1930 it was possible to perceive a profound change in the position of both countries regarding the rest of the world. Even before Roosevelt's time, there were some aspects that he would incorporate more powerfully and brilliantly into his Good Neighbor Policy. With respect to Europe the United States was sending observers and delegates to various organizations of the League of Nations, although without ever entering into the League itself. The North American reencounter with universal politics was expressed through Secretary of State Kellogg in the Pact of Paris of 1928, which bears his name together with that of French Minister Aristide Briand.

For her part Argentina, in the years following the Revolution of 1930, reincorporated herself with appropriate, vigorous ideas into international politics. Argentina took an active part in the peace negotiations between Paraguay and Bolivia, returned in 1933 to the League of Nations, carried out a plan of visits of chiefs of state, and participated in the Pan-American meetings.

On the international scene the Argentine attitude was to be so distinguished that she would enter into open rivalry with the United States for domination in the conduct of the hemisphere.

RETURN TO GENEVA

On March 10, 1919, the American Commission for the Negotiation of Peace invited the Argentine government, through its Minister Alvear in Paris, to participate in a conference wherein the victorious powers would examine the basis for the future League of Nations and also consider Argentine opinion in this respect. The telegraphic authorization from Foreign Minister Pueyrredón to Alvear contained, nevertheless, two observations:

first, the inconvenience of discussing these themes in private meetings; second, the idea that the distinction between belligerents and neutrals was no longer of any importance.

A new dispatch from Pueyrredón informed our minister in Paris that the executive power had decided to adhere without reservations to the pact of the League of Nations. On July 18 Alvear carried out these instructions, assuming the ratification on the part of Congress. The secretary of the League, James Eric Drummond, answered Alvear's note to the effect that the ratification of the Treaty of Versailles ought to precede the ratification of the pact; the Argentine adherence was premature but, at any rate, it would be held for an opportune time. Thus on January 10, 1920, Georges Clemenceau renewed the invitation to President Yrigoyen, and the latter renewed the adherence six days later. The executive branch sought and obtained agreement from the Senate for three Argentine delegates to the League of Nations: the foreign minister, Pueyrredón, and the ministers in Paris and Vienna, Alvear and Fernando Pérez, respectively. The instructions included a proposal regarding the the quality of states (victorious and conquered) as well as another on the designation of Council members by democratic methods. The logical failure of these proposals provoked the withdrawal of the Argentine delegation on December 2, 1920.

In June 1923 Alvear, now president of the Republic, sent to Congress a proposal of law according to which adherence to the League of Nations would be approved and our financial situation within the League regularized. Congress introduced a corresponding item into the budget law, but it did not approve the adherence to the League. Three other messages from Alvear had no better success. In 1926 the executive branch designated Tomás le Breton to the League of Nations, and two years later José María Cantilo carried out identical functions.

Under Yrigoyen's second presidency, the ties with the League were broken again, and the payment of dues was withheld.

Then came the Revolution of 1930; but the Provisional government took no initiative in this respect, because the Provisional President Uriburu was publicly against the League.

In 1932 the Justo government commissioned Ernesto Bosch to undertake negotiations with the League of Nations in order to clarify the Argentine position. Our country, with four years' unpaid dues, was the principal debtor within the international organization. The government, which was trying to repudiate Pueyrredón's act and at the same time to free itself from the large sum owing, pretended that our adherence, because of the lack of congressional ratification, had never been completed. With great lucidity Lisandro de la Torre opposed in the Senate the official chicanery.

Since our country had not adhered at the time of Yrigoyen, her entry now would necessitate a two-thirds' vote of the League members. Avoiding this dilemma, Law Number 11,752 approved in 1933 the pact of the League of Nations and provided for payment of a single quota. Article 5 of the law declared:

> In communicating this law to the Secretariat of the League of Nations, the executive branch will make evident that the Republic of Argentina considers that the Monroe Doctrine, mentioned by way of example in Article 21 of the pact, is a unilateral declaration, which in its time lent distinguished service to the cause of American emancipation, but which does not constitute a regional agreement as the mentioned article expresses it.

Thus the objection already presented in the meeting of the League by the Argentine delegate Cantilo was reproduced here.

After a haphazard and colorful negotiation, Argentina at last incorporated herself into the League, whose universality it would invoke very soon against the first attempts to perfect Pan-Americanism.

BRIEF WAR FOR PEACE

The first skirmish in the Argentine-North American rivalry would be set in motion paradoxically in connection with the attempts at peace in the war of Paraguay against Bolivia, in which both Argentina and the United States would dispute the initiative in negotiations tending to produce a solution for that bloody conflict. This had originated in the ambitions of both countries over a zone in litigation, the Chaco Boreal. Hostilities endured a long time, without reaching the point of formal declaration of war, and were limited to isolated encounters on the border.

The special conference on arbitration, which met in Washington in 1928 and 1929 in order to produce a solution for conflict, had created a commission of neutrals made up of five countries that did not border on the belligerents: United States, Columbia, Cuba, Mexico, and Uruguay. From this negotiation Argentina was excluded by the circumstance of not having attended the Washington conference. At the same time Secretary of State Stimson on August 3, 1932, extended to the continent the doctrine of nonrecognition of territorial conquests achieved by force, which the United States had already applied in the case of Manchuria, formulating it in the following terms: "The American nations further declare that they will not recognize any territorial arrangements of this controversy which have not been obtained through peaceful means nor the validity of territorial acquisitions which may be obtained through occupation or conquest by the force of arms."

The Argentine government three days later adhered to this declaration, but without prejudice, by organizing in its turn a commission parallel to that of the neutrals—made up of the following border countries: Argentina, Brazil, Chile, and Peru —which became known as the ABCP. On September 22 the same year the commission of neutrals proposed to Bolivia

and Paraguay that they agree to terminate hostilities immediately, and that they submit their disputes to arbitration. They
were also to accept a delegation designated for this purpose,
which would be charged with the duty of observing compliance
with arbitration. Furthermore, communications were sent to the
remaining American countries proposing to them that where-
ever the delegation might establish a violation of the armistice
by one of the belligerents, the violator would be considered an
aggressor—after which all diplomatic and consular representa-
tions should be immediately withdrawn from that country.

Hence the conflict was thus "Pan-Americanized," and the
faculty of resolving it was attributed to the commission of neutrals with its headquarters in Washington, to which our country
was opposed. This attempt was frustrated by Argentina, and
Saavedra Lamas instructed Espil as follows: ". . . this chancery
will not accompany the commission of neutrals in any act which,
passing beyond the limits of good offices and of the moral
influence of the opinions of all the continent, could approximate an intervention, even though this [intervention] might be
merely diplomatic, because such an attitude would be contrary
to Argentine tradition and doctrine. . . ."

Nor would he admit the collective intervention of all the
American countries attributable to the lack of a legal instrument
in this respect; he further reflected on the following: ". . . convenience of creating, not for the present Paraguayian-Bolivian
conflict but for the future, a pacific instrument or antiwar pact
which, linked to that of the League of Nations with others of
equal character existing in the world, might tend to guarantee
the reign of peace in a regime of conciliation, which would
not disallow but only complement and harmonize all of the
existing agreements."

He concluded with a new attempt to remit the conflict to the
League system, that is, to exclude it from Pan-American consideration: "I understand that the adoption of coercive measures

can only be founded on a treaty accepted in advance by the countries to which it is to be applied, as happens with the pact of the League of Nations, and that a simple declaration like that of August 3 is not sufficient to produce comminatory effects against third powers."

According to North American historian Bemis, this note would be attenuated in its expression by Ambassador Espil when he delivered it to the commission of neutrals.

The commission replied November 4 that it was not a question of coercive measures, but rather a new proposal to Bolivia and Paraguay, so that they might accept an authorization of peace without neglecting a sanction for whoever might violate it. The violator would be considered an aggressor, and diplomatic agents would be withdrawn—that is, if the belligerents would accept, it would be equivalent to an agreement with its own force.

Argentina rejected this consideration, in view of what was immediately pointed out:

> The commission of neutrals is notoriously lacking in every sense of political power and is not an international person with political attributions to pronounce in this respect. It is only a meeting of friendly countries united in an action of highest pacific inspiration, which honors them as well as the other American countries who have joined them, and whose limit of action is rigorously circumscribed to that of good offices.

And he again insisted on the jurisdiction of the League of Nations and on his repudiation of the Monroe Doctrine:

> In such sense, this chancery understands that the League of Nations has in this emergency a field of action established by the will of the conflicting parties themselves, who are signatories to its constitutive pact. And if the League acts in accordance with the purpose that inspires us all, we are also

of the opinion that this action [that is, of the League] can and must develop without the obstacle of regional or continental doctrine; but on our part, we see the necessity of making clear that they have not had the Argentine adherence, or a consecration established by the unanimous will of countries in the continent.

In this battle of influences seeking to resolve the conflict, Argentina would not tolerate the fact that Washington remained mistress of the solution; a century after the Monroe Doctrine Argentina utilized Europe (the League of Nations) to be counterposed to the United States (commission of neutrals). In this policy Argentina met complete success, for the commission of neutrals became dissolved; its communication to that effect did not conceal the interferences that motivated its failure:

. . . in view of present negotiations elsewhere between Bolivia and Paraguay for a settlement of the Chaco question, the commission of neutrals had nothing more to do in the affair and could contribute best to the establishment of peace by withdrawing from the situation the very object it had in view throughout the long, vexatious and patiently endured negotiations. Experience has demonstrated that when there is more than one center of negotiation, confusion and lack of agreement are the inevitable results . . . in this way the negotiations can be concentrated in Geneva, if other agents of peace adopt a similar attitude, permitting the League committee universal support in its effort toward peace.

The League of Nations having been rejected by Bolivia, the solution then remained in the hands of the ABCP, and in last instance with Argentina—in whose capital they were to undertake the first meetings for the Treaty of Peace early in 1935. The Argentine triumph was total in these activities, and Saavedra Lamas would later boast of the success of his antihemispheric policy: "We did not need to create any complicated enlargement, any complex international structure, to confine the dispute to its own center."

Argentina, in its opposition to Washington's commission of neutrals, had underscored the nonexistence of prior agreements for the effective solution of the Bolivian-Paraguayan war. In order to fill this gap outside the Pan-American system, Argentina proposed the famous Antiwar Pact.

While it was contributing to the downfall of the commission of neutrals, the Argentine Foreign Office hastened to take the lead in a bellicose campaign for peace. There was no other point to the South American Antiwar Pact—projected, from the one side, behind the back of the United States and, on the other, open to universal adherence of all nations. Argentina opposed attempts to Pan-Americanize the peace efforts by trying to insert its treaty within the framework of the League of Nations.

After criticizing, in the exposition of motives, the irreducible opposition between the Saxon and the Latin within the Pan American system, only public opinion was admitted in the text as a sanction, and advantage was taken to proscribe every kind of intervention, whether armed or merely diplomatic. With the paragraph against intervention, Argentina took revenge for her failure in the Sixth Conference in Havana in 1928.

The program for the coming Montevideo Conference was already being prepared. Argentina obtained in May 1933—with due respect to the proposal of Chile—that the antiwar project be included in the agenda of the Conference. However, that this pact was ratified by six countries was qualified by historian Bemis as a "notable blow." On occasion of President Justo's visit to Brazil October 10, 1933, Argentina, Brazil, Chile, Mexico, Paraguay, and Uruguay formalized their adherence to the work of Saavedra Lamas. Thus, not with a mere project to be discussed, but with a treaty already ratified by the most important Latin American countries, Argentina could present herself in the Montevideo Conference with the most solid basis of negotiation.

Meanwhile, North American elections were favoring the

Democratic candidate, Franklin D. Roosevelt, who in his campaign had announced a new deal for the Latin American republics, the Good Neighbor Policy.

THE APOGEE OF ARGENTINE PRESTIGE

The United States, however, attended the Montevideo meeting only with good intentions; Argentina came with a consummated fact. The conference was to be held in 1932 but had been postponed. The enthusiasm of the new North American administration had succeeded in avoiding any further postponements, but the atmosphere was hardly that of optimism: it was believed that the United States sought compensation in the hemisphere for her failures in the London and Geneva conferences. The Roosevelt government not only insisted that the meeting take place, but also, for the first time in the case of such a conference held outside Washington, it sent its secretary of state as head of the delegation.

Cordell Hull, a Southern Puritan, who believed in citing the Old Testament and the War of the Secession as means of solving contemporary problems, was disposed to play a modest but active role in Montevideo.

He did not oppose anything or take part in debates; he spoke only a few times, and his interventions were brief but to the point. He did not preside over any of the nine commissions or try in any way to assume the direction of anything. This, according to Bemis, he left to the Argentine delegation, headed by Dr. Saavedra Lamas. But his tireless action was carried out in the anterooms, in corridors, and in hotel rooms, as Gerchunoff records in the accounts he wrote from Montevideo for *La Nación:* "Mr. Hull visits his colleagues from America; he chats soberly and amiably with them—always a pencil in his hand; he evidently hopes that Mr. Roosevelt's policy will make people forget the policy of Mr. Coolidge."

Argentina, as Hull himself records, after emphatically, though unsuccessfully, proposing the postponement of the conference, arrived at the last moment and installed its delegation outside the Uruguayan capital, in the luxury hotel of Carrasco. There, patiently, Hull betook himself. The Argentine delegation was composed of Juan F. Cafferata, Ramón S. Castillo, Isidoro Ruiz Moreno, Raúl Prebisch, Carlos Brebbia, Luis Podestá Costa, Daniel Antokoletz, and Alejandro M. Unsain. They could not conceal their surprise over the visit from the United States' secretary of state. Saavedra Lamas was equally astonished when Hull, after referring to Saavedra as the principal Latin American statesman and after asking him for advice, informed him that his country was disposed to sign the Antiwar Pact. Ambassador Espil had already dropped the word in Washington that this kind of gesture was the surest way to win the heart of Saavedra Lamas. Hull proposed that he [Saavedra Lamas] should pronounce a solemn discourse in order to present the peace motion, and Hull also promised him his support. Saavedra Lamas looked at him and smoked nervously. In order to convince him, Hull added that if this did not appear in order, he would then yield to the person next in line. The Argentine chancellor asked for a day to consider it. Before twenty-four hours had elapsed, he returned Hull's visit and informed him that he was in accord. With a smile he commented: "We shall be the two wings of the dove of peace—you the economic, and I the political."

This was because Saavedra Lamas had pledged himself to support the economic proposal presented by the North American delegation, although his government did not look favorably upon certain points that were involved. In fact, Argentina snubbed the Mexican proposal for public debt moratoriums, and in a long speech it was made known that she surrendered to the North American position in economic matters. At this moment both countries were coinciding in their economic policy, as the New York Times pointed out on December 9, 1933, since both had resorted to the same methods in order to adjust their public finances: opposition to the monetary pattern and provisional stabilization of exchanges; preference for bilateral treaties with immediate adjustment, inasmuch as they could not achieve this true multilateral instrument. A few days earlier, a comparable situation in the United States was evidenced in the creation of the Grain Board and in the norms for exchanges according to the National Recovery Act.

In view of these political parallels of recovery the Mexican proposal could not satisfy our country, for it had just made great sacrifices in order to maintain service on the external debt. The consequent animadversion of Mexico was translated into a proposal to postpone indefinitely the meetings of the economic commission that had been created through the initiative of Saavedra Lamas.

All the witnesses pointed out the relaxation of tension in the relations between Argentina and the United States. The only exception was Argentina's pro forma participation in the debate on nonintervention, whereby Saavedra Lamas pronounced only the indispensable words. As they were leaving the session, Hull sought him out and greeted him saying: "I know there was nothing else you could have done in the circumstances," for which the Argentine chancellor thanked him smilingly.

The Argentine-North American honeymoon made possible the success of the Seventh Conference, but at the same time it aroused the jealousy of Brazil. Hull reports in his memoirs that one of his most delicate tasks was to relieve the Brazilian worry over the flourishing friendship with Argentina. In Montevideo, the Brazilian foreign minister, Mello Franco, had manifested his displeasure over the belief that Hull was consulting Saavedra Lamas too much. It took the North American government a long time to tranquilize our susceptible neighbor.

THE BUENOS AIRES MEETING

The dilatory transactions for peace in the Chaco finally succeeded in halting hostilities, and an armistice was signed June

14, 1935, in the Palacio San Martin of the Argentine capital. However, the final conditions of peace were not subscribed to until July 1938.

In January 1936 President Roosevelt wrote a letter to General Justo, proposing an extraordinary inter-American conference, and if the Argentine government were willing, it would take place in Buenos Aires. Roosevelt justified this personal gesture, made outside the usual diplomatic channels, by alluding to the "vital importance" of the questions for the American peoples. In other words, this he felt would be the best form of maintaining peace among the American republics, whether through the prompt ratification of instruments already negotiated or through modification of the same, or through the creation of new instruments.

After the Argentine acceptance, the date was set in December 1936 and, once Roosevelt had been elected, Justo invited him to the inauguration of the conference. The principal point in the program was the organization of peace, while the other themes referred to neutrality, arms limitation, juridical problems, economic problems and intellectual cooperation. Underlying all was the North American design to accelerate steps toward perfecting the hemispheric system.

President Roosevelt arrived aboard the cruiser *Indianapolis* on November 30, and his presence aroused a warm popular reception. The North American delegation, headed by Hull, was as follows: Sumner Welles; the North American ambassador at Buenos Aires, Alexander W. Wedell; Adolf A. Berle; and Charles G. Fenwick. Our delegation, headed by Saavedra Lamas, included Roberto M. Ortiz, Miguel Angel Cárcano, José María Cantilo, Felipe A. Espil, Leopoldo Melo, Isidoro Ruiz Moreno, and Daniel Antokoletz. The Argentine alternates were Carlos Brebbia and César Díaz Cisneros. In the inaugural session the President of the United States spoke, as well as the President of Argentina. Justo utilized a phrase of Baron Río

Branco to affirm the ties with Europe, and in referring to the program of the assembly he added:

It appears unnecessary to insist that in the realization of these noble purposes there is no thought of creating antagonistic continental groups. We aspire only to finding the most perfect formulas for the pacific settlement of international disputes that will merit the support of all the nations.

He continued with a paragraph that advocated solidarity with the League of Nations. These principles prefigure the position that the Argentine delegation would adopt regarding the fundamental problems.

In his reply, Roosevelt, on the contrary, insisted on hemispheric unity and the system of consultation:

In this determination to live at peace among ourselves we in the Américas make it at the same time clear that we stand shoulder to shoulder in our final determination that others who, driven by war madness or land hunger, might seek to commit acts of aggression against us, will find a hemisphere wholly prepared to consult together for our mutual safety and our mutual good.

The most important debates took place in the first commission of the Conference, that of organization for peace. Roosevelt's letter, which had been the origin of the Conference, alluded to the necessity of ratifying existing treaties of peace if a convenience of reforming them was not indicated. There were five agreements: the treaty to avoid and prevent conflicts (called "Gondra," Santiago de Chile, 1923); the Kellogg-Briand Pact (Paris, 1928); the Inter-American Treaties of Conciliation and Arbitration (Washington, 1929); and the South American Antiwar Pact (called "Saavedra Lamas," Rio de Janeiro, 1933). Argentina had ratified the last.

Immediately Brazil asked that each country relate the reasons impeding ratification of the instruments of peace. Some delegates formulated statements, but Argentina and the United States kept silent. Three days later, in an intervention during the session, Saavedra Lamas resumed the peculiar posture of Argentina:

> A disturbed and agitated world surrounds us. There are dense clouds on its horizon; at times lightning flashes, and perhaps a great storm will come. But this storm will find us united, disposed to noble consultation and to interchange of ideas for the protection of our continent from repercussions that we cannot admit. This will turn us also toward all the horizons and will offer the collaboration and cooperation that we are disposed to extend to the great human ideals—ideals having no limits or continental restrictions.

Apart from this intervention wherein—in keeping with the meteorological metaphors—the Argentine resistance to a too narrowly conceived continental action became spelled out, our delegation through Antokoletz and Saavedra Lamas tried to universalize the organization of peace with juridical arguments against the existence of an American regional international law. For the Argentine chancellor, to have a greater regional organization would be to "create within the world a great Robinson Crusoe's island." Argentina also adhered to the proposal of postponing a project for creating an inter-American court of justice.

On December 7, 1936, Hull proposed a resolution to strengthen peace in the hemisphere. His proposal sought to coordinate the five existing conventions. Also in the case of a threat to the peace of the hemisphere, it established a system of compulsory consultation among the foreign ministers, for which there was created a permanent Inter-American Consultative Committee.

Saavedra Lamas had drafted a proposal of voluntary collaboration with the measures and sanctions of the League of Nations that were to apply to the states which had accepted the Kellogg-Briand Pact or the Antiwar Pact, or both. Consultation was established for instances of violation of principles and/or obligations pertaining to the existing inter-American treaties of peace. Finally, nonintervention was stipulated with an express condemnation of any excessive diplomatic intervention.

Hull's project created an inter-American organism of compulsory competence in conflicts, while that of Lamas was opposed to it, and he underscored the principle of nonintervention in the most absolute form. The divergence between the projects deepened the latent discord between the ministers of Argentina and the United States. The honeymoon of Montevideo had faded away rapidly. In his memoirs, Hull recalls the hostility expressed by Saavedra Lamas—his strong words in a succession of meanings, each time more agitated—and that upon Hull's departure from Buenos Aires the Argentine chancellor refrained from the "usual courtesy of seeing me off."

Saavedra Lamas, then at the pinnacle of prestige, in Geneva had presided over the assembly of the League of Nations and had also become a recipient of the Nobel Peace Prize. According to Sumner Welles, Saavedra Lamas early in the conference attempted to impose his will on the Central American delegates. But the interview, which took place in his private residence, had terminated abruptly.

The Brazilian delegation found the solution for the Argentine-North American divergence. This delegation was headed by José Carlos de Macedo Soares, and Oswaldo Aranha, who presented a project uniting the principle of consultation with that of nonintervention—both of which were finally sanctioned in two distinct instruments. The first was the Convention for the Maintenance, Preservation, and Reestablishment of Peace, whose dispositive part declares:

Article 1: In the event that the peace of the American Republics is menaced, and in order to coordinate efforts to prevent war, any of the Governments of the American Republics signatory to the Treaty of Paris of 1928 or to the Treaty of Non-Aggression and Conciliation of 1933, or to both, whether or not a member of other peace organizations, shall consult with other Governments of the American Republics, which, in such event, shall consult together for the purpose of finding and adopting methods of peaceful cooperation.

Article 2: In the event of war, or a virtual state of war between American States, the Governments of the American Republics represented at this Conference shall undertake without delay, the necessary mutual consultations, in order to exchange views and to seek, within the obligations resulting from the pacts above mentioned and from the standards of international morality, a method of peaceful collaboration; and, in the event of an international war outside America which might menace the peace of the American Republics, such consultation shall also take place to determine the proper time and manner in which the signatory states, if they so desire, may eventually cooperate in some action tending to preserve the peace of the American Continent.

The phrase "if they so desire" was, according to Hull, an Argentine means of weakening the resolution.

The second instrument was the Additional Protocol Relative to Nonintervention, which declared:

Article 1: The High Contracting Parties declare inadmissible the intervention of any one of them, directly or indirectly, and for whatever reason, in the internal or external affairs of any other of the Parties.

The violation of the provisions of this Article shall give rise to mutual consultation, with the object of exchanging views and seeking methods of peaceful adjustment.

The discussion of these texts—which, on account of their importance as a base of inter-American organization, are reproduced in full—does not emerge from the minutes of the Conference, but rather from the debate regarding the Declaration of

Principles of Inter-American Solidarity and Cooperation, the keystone of that organization.

Argentina rejected the idea of an American association. Cantilo hastened to formulate an opinion regarding the lack of maturity in a project creating a "political organism exclusively American with permanent character." "I believe that that is the the general idea," he said. Saavedra Lamas, who called the system of consultation "a walking Pan American Union," proposed on his part that the theme pass to the next conference at Lima.

The original text of the treaty dealing with solidarity, which had been edited by the Central American nations included an article to provide explicitly for a common reaction of the American nations against an extracontinental attack on any country of the hemisphere:

> Article 2: All the nations of the hemisphere will consider as an attack upon themselves any attack that may be inflicted by extracontinental nations on the rights of any one of them—the attack giving rise to a uniform and common reaction. In this event, the Foreign Ministries of the American nations will proceed to an immediate agreement in order to determine the measures that the situation demands.

The text, however, as presented to the first commission, had already been profoundly modified. The allusion to the extracontinental attack had disappeared, and it became watered down to such vague terms:

> Article 2: All the American nations will consider as an attack upon themselves any attack that may be inflicted by any nation on the rights of another—necessarily giving rise to an agreement or a consultation among the Foreign Ministries of those affected, in order to determine the attitude to be taken or, on occasion, the rules to be adopted for the neutrality agreed upon.

It is evident that the revised draft detracted from the sense of

the original project. In its new form the article also included
attacks carried out by all countries of the hemisphere. But still
the Argentine delegation was not satisfied. It was necessary then
to give up the treaty and to elaborate a declaration whose
principal paragraph stated the following:

> Article 2: Every act of unfriendly nature, with respect to any
> one of them, that is capable of disturbing the peace affects
> each one and all of them. Such act justifies the initiation of
> procedures of consultation, as provided in the December 1936
> Convention for the Maintenance, Preservation, and Reestab-
> lishment of Peace.

Even with this curtailed text our delegation asked a postponement in order to receive instructions, which move brought forth
from the Brazilian delegate, Aranha, this commentary: "We
desire to create a force by unanimity, and we are going to wait;
our waiting will prove that every time we must wait for Argentina, time is not lost."

At last, the Argentine representatives consented to subscribe
to the fourth draft:

> Article 2: That every act susceptible of disturbing the peace
> of America affects each and every one of them, and justifies
> the initiation of the procedure of consultation provided for
> in the Convention for the Maintenance, Preservation, and
> Reestablishment of Peace, signed at this Conference. . . .

Other paragraphs of the declaration proclaimed republican,
democractic, and sovereign principles, as well as others appropriate to the American community such as proscription of territorial conquest, condemnation of intervention, illegality of
forced collection of debts, and resort to conciliation and arbitration.

The Argentine reticence toward every compromise that might
consolidate hemispheric unity, as revealed in this long struggle,

would also be manifest toward whatever individual initiative might lead to that goal. Thus, Antokoletz succeeded in obtaining that the treaty on good offices and mediation was not obligatory. Finally, our country tried through this same delegate to "universalize" the instruments so laboriously concluded, that is, to open them to "the universal adherence of all states" and to dilute or dissolve Pan-Americanism within the system. With this a clamor of opposition arose, and the voice of the American delegation—until then mute because the North Americans had not intervened in the earlier discussions—warned emphatically of treaties that could not be open to the adherence of non-American countries because of their essential character.

The North Americans immediately made clear that they were referring to the three most important instruments achieved by the conference: that for the maintenance of peace, for nonintervention, and for solidarity.

A CRUISER IN THE PACIFIC

In August 1938 the Peruvian Foreign Ministry invited the other nations of America to the Eighth International Conference of American States, which was to open in Lima December 9. The world panorama then was even darker than in the time of the Buenos Aires meeting. Alliances among the countries forming the Axis, along with the territorial expansions of a Germany rapidly rearming under the direction of Hitler, aroused a concern that even the Munich meeting in September had not been able to alleviate.

In this conference Argentina adopted a peevish attitude. In Rome, as early as March 4, José María Cantilo, before leaving the Embassy in Italy to become foreign minister, had proposed to to the other American countries that the Lima meeting be postponed for one or two years. Our delegation was not headed by the foreign minister but by the legal counselor, Isidoro Ruiz

Moreno, and was composed of Adrián C. Escobar, Horacio Rivarola, Mario Antelo, César Díaz Cisneros, Ricardo Marcó del Pont, and Alejandro Bunge.

While Hull, once again heading his delegation, was approaching Lima aboard the *Santa Clara*, he received a wireless message from Rio de Janeiro wherein Foreign Minister Aranha informed him that Cantilo in his inaugural speech proposed to reject the idea of a collective security pact. For, although the Argentine chancellor was not a member of his delegation, he had not lost the opportunity to inaugurate the new cruiser *La Argentina*, recently acquired in Italy, in order to travel to Lima—thus copying Roosevelt's visit to Buenos Aires—and to pronounce a speech at the opening of the conference from which he was to withdraw at once.

Upon arriving, Hull immediately requested an interview with Cantilo, but the results were not satisfactory. But the United States secretary of state delivered to his Argentine colleague a copy of the declaration prepared by the North American delegation.

As was speculated, J. M. Cantilo's speech, though it did contain a paragraph of compromise on hemispheric unity, turned out to be a most passionate defense of the Latin American links to Europe:

> American solidarity, gentlemen, is a fact which no one can or does put in doubt. Each and every one of us is disposed to uphold and to approve this solidarity in the face of any danger, wherever it may come from, that may threaten the independence or the sovereignty of any state of this part of the world. For this we do not need any special pacts. The pact has already been made by our history. We would act with a single and identical impulse, our territorial borders wiped out and under a single flag for all—the flag of liberty and justice.

Apart from the lack of necessity for treaties, American solidarity as seen by Cantilo was supported by the most profound national individualism:

> But Argentina believes that each American people, with its distinctive character, ought to develop its own policy without forgetting thereby the great continental solidarity or the natural gravitation of reciprocal interests that are grouped by reason of geography.

To these reservations, which practically annulled every principle of continental solidarity, there followed the most coherent formulation of the link with Europe:

> It must be said that our continental solidarity cannot be exclusive of what unites us to the rest of the human race, and that we cannot be disinterested in what occurs outside America. Argentina has not done so and will not do so, not only for reasons in the economic sphere, but also for historical considerations as well as those of sentimental character.

Within the reasoning of Cantilo, the argument is true and in anticipation it refutes the interpretations that would reduce our traditional admiration for Europe to a mere economic determinism. In continuation there occurs a paragraph which is a forerunner of the opinions of Ruiz Guiñazú on Pearl Harbor:

> Just as the United States maintained the Open Door Policy in China, was moved to interest herself in the Hawaiian Islands, and then after the 1898 war with Spain obtained the cession of the Philippine Islands—a policy that was not exclusively American—so the interests, and not Argentina's alone, held by the River Plate countries in the European markets are in opposition and do carry weight in their national and international policies. But here economic reasons are not necessarily of paramount importance in determining the course of Argentine international policy. We feel a close solidarity with Europe through the immigration we received from that continent, an element that has contributed so much to our greatness; also to European capital we owe the develop-

ment of our agricultural production, of our railroads and industries. Even beyond this, our mind is impregnated with the memory of the men who had discovered and populated these lands and with the cultural tradition they had bequeathed to us. From Spain came our race and religion, while from France, Great Britain, and the United States came the doctrinal orientation of our democratic institutions. If to the mother country we owe the basis of our literature, then to French culture we owe the basic formation of our intellectual life and to Italy and Germany all the vital aspects of our evolution. Hence the predominating influence in our educational system and in our universities is European. This influence obviously affects the international policy of Argentina as it does, I am sure, that of all Latin peoples of this continent; in the same way the interests of the British Empire are cherished and must be cherished by our brothers in the north.

And he could not fail, before concluding, to link this ideology with an allusion to the posture Roque Sáenz Peña had assumed a half century earlier in the first inter-American conference:

> Thus stands determined the attitude which the Argentine delegation is to adopt in this conference, but nothing of this is to sink us into unilateral and sectarian exclusivisms. Universalism, the ecumenical spirit, is the tradition in the country of him who one day in Washington had expounded the motto of Argentine international policy as "America for humanity."

Two days later, aboard his brand new cruiser, Cantilo left Lima en route to the Chilean lakes, where he would complete his vacation. The Argentine delegation remained in the hands of Ruiz Moreno, whom Cantilo ordered not to enter into any agreement without consulting him first—a · requirement that would be difficult to meet, as will be proved later on.

Neither Argentina nor the United States officially presented their proposals for a declaration in the commissions of the conference; however, they discussed them in interminable meetings lasting ten days thereafter, meetings which Hull remembers as "among the most difficult of my career." The North American project favored a firm American solidarity in spite of the extra-continental threats it had to confront. The Argentine delegation was in opposition and had rejected every decision that might impair its European stand. As the negotiations lagged, a meeting was called in the quarters of the Brazilian delegation. The Argentine representative insisted on his thesis, while the Uruguayan and Chilean delegates supported him partially with respect to the possible commercial consequences of the declaration. Hull presented a suggestion from Roosevelt, stated in energetic language, which alarmed various delegates. To this Ruiz Moreno replied by proposing a project that would embrace the threats from non-American governments or from any other governments, or that would indeed fail to make mention of these distinctions. The first possibility alluded to the United States and the second was inoperative. The discussion continued until very late and became somewhat heated; however, except for Argentina, an agreement was reached on the reference to non-American governments, with resultant unanimity in pointing to the activities of penetration, as well as to the use of force or the use of a mere threat. Ruiz Moreno resorted to telegraphing Buenos Aires for further instructions.

Hull, on his part, in search of a solution to the conflict, resorted to a direct telephone communication with President Ortiz. Even from the Casa Rosada he found it difficult to contact the vacationing foreign minister. Finally, from the Chilean lakes, Cantilo sent Ruiz Moreno a new proposal for declaration similar to that which Hull had given him in Lima, except that it did not provide for a regular system of meetings of foreign ministers.

When agreement was reached with regard to Cantilo's proposal, a new difficulty arose. On Mello Franco's initiative Presidents Vargas and Ortiz had joined in another proposal, which they likewise sent to Lima. Hull personally had to convince them to withdraw it, so that it might not interfere with that now being shared by the delegates.

The result of these battered transactions was the document known as the Declaration of Lima, unanimously approved on Christmas eve. Its text is the following:

The Governments of the American States
Declare:

First. That they reaffirm their continental solidarity and their purpose to collaborate in the maintenance of the principles upon which the said solidarity is based.

Second. That faithful to the above-mentioned principles and to their absolute sovereignty, they reaffirm their decision to maintain them and to defend them against all foreign intervention or activity that may threaten them.

Third. And in case the peace, security, or territorial integrity of any American Republic is thus threatened by acts of any nature that may impair them, they proclaim their common concern and their determination to make effective their solidarity, coordinating their respective sovereign wills by means of the procedure of consultation, established by conventions in force and by declarations of the Inter-American Conferences, using the measures which in each case the circumstances may make advisable. It is understood that the Governments of the American Republics will act independently in their individual capacity, recognizing fully their juridical equality as sovereign states.

Fourth. That in order to facilitate the consultations established in this and other American peace instruments, the Ministers for Foreign Affairs of the American Republics, when deemed desirable and at the initiative of any one of them, will meet in their several capitals by rotation and without protocolary character. Each Government may, under special circumstances or for special reasons, designate a representative as a substitute for its Minister for Foreign Affairs.

Certain journalistic commentaries emphasized the circumstance that only a declaration had been obtained, not a treaty. In his memoirs, Hull, who seemed satisfied with the definitive text, explains that he preferred a declaration with immediate effect and without the necessity of later ratification, to a treaty more cautiously worded that would have wound up in the archives of a foreign ministry or of a congressional committee, never to be ratified.

Irrespective of the grumblers, Argentina had adhered to this declaration which was sensibly advancing the inter-American system, but by no means was she renouncing thereby her links to Europe. These strong ideological and commercial links in some way have contributed to Argentina's obstructionist attitude manifested in the last conferences, which founded a system soon to be tested in war.

3: THE WAR

The German invasion of Poland unleashed the biggest conflict in history. The first Argentine reaction was a decree of September 4, 1939, which declared the Republic's neutrality in the presently existing state of war, with express reference to the Hague conventions of 1899 and 1907, although the latter, as usual, were lacking the required ratification from the Argentine Congress.

The following day the British Embassy in Buenos Aires listed the articles considered as contraband of war. Among the items classed as "conditional contraband" were foods in general, food products, animal feeds, forage, clothing, and the materials used in their production. On September 8 Foreign Minister Cantilo offered all the necessary reservations with respect to the products of "conditional contraband," since they would affect the "exportation of a series of food articles proper to Argentine production." Two days later the Foreign Office made known the English decision to facilitate inoffensive neutral commerce without prejudice to prevention of contraband articles reaching the enemy. The decision regarded with sympathy the indications of the neutrals on commerce of good faith. The German government also tried to put limitations on trade, which aroused a consequent Argentine protest.

When the cruiser division of the Argentine navy, under the command of Rear Admiral José Guisasola, had visited Rio de Janeiro, it was most opportune for this high official to consult

50

with the Brazilian Foreign Ministry. There he was informed of the rules of neutrality of the Rio government, and it was settled that both countries would attend the forthcoming conference of Panama in common agreement. The agenda advanced by the United States was satisfactory, and there was no necessity to modify it. Shortly afterward, a Brazilian envoy would fly to Buenos Aires on a similar mission.

PANAMA, 1939

When the Second World War broke out, almost simultaneously the government of the United States decided to convoke the First Meeting of Consultation of the American Foreign Ministers, in accordance with the system designed in Lima the year before, and for the purpose of exchanging points of view "as the measures they may collectively or individually take in order best to assure the peace of the American continent." Argentina accepted the invitation but instructed its delegate, Leopoldo Melo, to avoid political and military commitments and to urge that debates of the conference be limited to the juridical and economic framework of the basic program. The agenda of the conference, worked out by the governing board of the Pan American Union, centered on three principal themes: neutrality, protection of peace in the hemisphere, and economic cooperation to ameliorate the effects of the war on the economies of the American countries.

The most spectacular result was the so-called Declaration of Panama, by which there was constituted a maritime security zone around the continent, whose extension varied between 300 and 1,000 miles. Within this "chastity belt" it was prohibited to the belligerents to carry out acts of war. The Argentine delegate, Melo, obtained that the patrolling of this zone should be of facultative character, but our country was not convinced of its utility. He also imposed the criterion that the declaration would lose its effect if a dissolving condition should evolve: the entrance of any American country into the war. This declaration had no more than a theoretical value, and on December 13 it was violated in the incident of the Graf Spee, in the course of which a German cruiser so named and three British cruisers sustained combat in front of the Uruguayan coast.

A new declaration of American solidarity and another on neutrality were also approved. The original draft of the latter theme prohibited the entrance of belligerents' submarines into neutral ports; however, on Argentine initiative, the definitive text delegated to the internal legislation of each country the attitude to be taken regarding the submarines. Argentina also succeeded in having included a reservation regarding the Falkland Islands situation.

But the most important point in the agenda—at least for the majority of the Latin American delegations, including ours—was that referring to compensating measures concerning the economic consequences of the war. Some of these countries, Argentina above all, depended almost completely on their exchange with European markets. With this flourishing commerce upset by the war, they sought solutions within the hemisphere, and hence the creation of the Inter-American Financial and Economic Advisory Committee—composed of twenty-one experts in economic affairs, one for each country—which began to function in Washington on November 15. This committee was to concern itself with studying economic problems arising from the war and with recommending methods for solving them.

The climate of the conference was exceptionally cordial. This circumstance must be credited to the fact that the United States admitted the initiatives of her Latin American neighbors and committed herself to greater cooperation with respect to economic problems. On the other hand, the conference Pan-Americanized in Panama the dogma of neutrality so dear to Argentine tradition that, furthermore, happened to coincide at the moment with the foreign policy of Washington.

The chief of the North American delegation, Sumner Welles, considered it necessary to "emphasize the altogether cooperative, helpful, and able services rendered during the meeting at Panama by the Argentine delegation, headed by Dr. Leopoldo Melo. Dr. Melo's long experience in the public life of his own country has caused him to be generally regarded as one of the elder statesmen of the Western Hemisphere, and at the meeting he consistently exercised his great ability to achieve practical and successful results. In fact, throughout the meeting there was not the slightest cloud upon the horizon of inter-American unity."

REVISION OF NEUTRALITY

In April 1940 the rhythm of the European hostilities had not acquired the intensity of the blitzkrieg period. People were still living through the ambiguous months to which the name of the phony war was given. The United States had just passed its fifth neutrality law (November 4, 1939), and its position regarding the conflict was still relatively withdrawn.

This was the moment that President Ortiz' Foreign Minister Cantilo chose to initiate discussions with the North American Ambassador Armour, for the purpose of revising the traditional concept of neutrality and replacing it with a more realistic notion that would lend itself more effectively to concrete facts. The Argentine attitude was made known officially by means of a circular to our embassies and legations, in which it was recalled that classical neutrality implied bilateral obligations and created rights, but also created reciprocal guarantees. In reality, something else was happening:

> But in the situation of today the belligerent states do not respect the will of the neutrals; nor can the latter make them respect their neutrality as a juridical form of their isolation. Neutrality, created to preserve a sovereignty, under the existing conditions is either ridiculed or belittled—and in no way protected. It is a fiction, a dead concept, which has to be

replaced within the reality of the times in which we are living.

He expressed also that the Declaration of Panama and the maritime security zone were the maximum forces in the observance of neutrality within the norms of international law. For Cantilo the permanent committee of Rio, which came into being along with those forces, was only a "wheel that turns in a vacuum." The Argentine proposal sought to overcome this fiction and to return to the nonbelligerents a position of legal strength, clearly related to reality—without the least intention, however, of bringing war to the continent. In brief, "the supreme interests of America ought to stimulate a circumstantial policy, and a policy coordinated with watchfulness ought to be opposed to the simply juridical concept of neutrality."

Paradoxically, this notable Argentine initiative did not find an echo in the United States. Sumner Welles indicated to Espil the dangers that so transcendental a declaration would involve for his government, especially since only a few months before Congress had approved a new neutrality law with norms they did not consider convenient to challenge or discuss. This sluggish attitude of the United States, which momentarily stood behind Argentina, was evidently determined by internal political circumstances. In particular, that northern country found itself submerged in a presidential election campaign, one of the most bitter and hard-fought in its history, in which Roosevelt's opposition once more played the cards of isolationism and insisted that the United States not be dragged into the war. Therefore, any suggestion of abandonment of neutrality would then appear electorally imprudent. Nevertheless, in practice, North American policy came closer every day to the formula proclaimed by Argentina.

This clear intent of our Foreign Ministry had no success in its own time, but later events would undertake to witness its prophetic opportunity. Unfortunately, the next changes in the

Argentine governmental teams would not only prevent the maintenance of this line but would also bog the country down in a neutralism that was evermore awkward and anachronistic.

HAVANA, 1940

Quite suddenly the European war gained momentum, and in a few days Belgium, France, and Holland fell into the hands of the Third Reich. England alone continued to resist. And with an Atlantic frontier that could be crossed, America's situation was becoming vulnerable.

Apart from the impression produced by the rapidity of these conquests, there arose a concrete problem in the American continent: the fate of the possessions of the two defeated European powers, France and Holland. The United States, therefore, immediately convoked the Second Meeting of the Foreign Ministers of the American Countries. This took place in Havana from July 21 to July 30, 1940.

Without prejudice to this measure, a month sooner on June 18 the Congress of the United States at the proposal of Hull unanimously approved a joint resolution: the United States would not recognize the transfer of any geographic region in this hemisphere from one non-American power to another non-American power; and in the event of a transfer or an attempted transfer, the United States would consult with the other American republics without excluding other measures to safeguard common interests.

The agenda of the conference can be summed up as the authorization of urgent defense measures in the face of possible transfer of territories; the subversive activities promoted from outside against the American republics, as well as the grave economic difficulties created by the war. The subversion theme was of special concern to the United States, in view of the recently experienced instances of fifth-column operations in the submission of the countries freshly conquered. Regarding territorial transfer, Washington foresaw two possibilities: one, that Germany itself might obtain bases a short distance from the Panama Canal: the other, that Germany might offer their colonies to one or more of the Latin American countries in exchange for a political and economic vassalage and thus might break up Pan-American solidarity.

The United States, through Hull, chief of the delegation, presented on the part of the American republics a project for collective trusteeship over the colonies and possessions of the European nations in America. The United States made plain, in order to avoid suspicions regarding the trusteeship, that there cannot be "linked to it the creation of special interests on the part of one American republic."

The Argentine delegation, again headed by Leopoldo Melo, formulated a series of objections to the proposal from the United States. The delegation maintained, with regard to the establishment of the collective trusteeship, that it referred more to persons than to goods, according to the juridical concepts of the common law. Therefore, it would be convenient to use a new term, such as "administration"—which finally was accepted —qualifying it with the adjective "provisional," in order to emphasize its precarious character and to maintain a transitory procedure. It was the aspect of the risk involved in the measures to be adopted that the Argentine delegation insisted upon most strongly.

In support of this position, it was required that the people of the territories be consulted before the new administration became implanted. In his memoirs Hull states that regarding the transfer of colonies Melo would not accept anything more than a declaration similar to that of the North American Congress, in the sense of not recognizing or agreeing to the transfer of territories. To strengthen his position, he affirmed that "any assumption of sovereignty by the American republics over territory of European powers in the Western Hemisphere was an act of war, and war in the case of Argentina could not be declared except by the Argentine Congress." On the other hand, Hull also records that Melo deemed any transfer of colonies as "hypothetical because the British fleet would keep the Germans out of the hemisphere."

At the same time, Melo took advantage of a pessimistic report from Admiral Stark to the United States House of Representatives, which had been made public in order to imply that if the North Americans could not defend themselves, as Stark's report suggested, much less could they go down 6,500 miles to defend their allies in the extreme south.

The discussions between Hull and Melo were extended to the point that the conference seemed to be reduced to a dialogue between those two delegates. It was so obvious that the New York Times, July 29, 1940, made an issue of this fact. It reported that negotiations over the problem of trusteeship between Secretary Hull and Señor Melo were that extensive and overpowering so as to cause dismay among the other delegates, who complained that it was in reality an "Argentine-North American meeting," and they were beginning to doubt the meaning of their own presence.

As the conference was making no headway, Hull decided to return to the methods he had used at Lima and, in agreement with Melo, he communicated directly with Acting President Castillo, who imparted the necessary instructions so that the Argentine delegation might go along with the majority.

The principal fruits of the conference were two documents oriented toward a single end: the nonrecognition of the transfer of territories between nonhemispheric powers. The first was the Convention on the Provisional Administration of European Colonies and Possessions in the Americas. It would enter into effect more slowly, because it required the parliamentary ratification by the signatory states; but, for the first time, the principle of unanimity was abandoned and was replaced by a provision making effective the two-thirds vote of the American republics. The treaty created an agency called the Inter-American Commission for Territorial Administration, composed of one representative from each of the states that might ratify the agreement.

While this instrument was being established through the required number of ratifications, it was necessary to provide for a more practical and flexible disposition that would not involve the laborious procedure of ratification. Accordingly, the second instrument was offered: the Act of Havana Concerning Provisional Administration of European Colonies and Possessions in the Americas, which set up an emergency committee composed of a representative from each one of the republics. It regarded the possibility "as an imperative emergency measure" to apply the stipulations of the aforementioned convention, or to act in the form that national defense might require on the part of "any of the American republics individually or jointly with others."

Another instrument, which in spite of reiterating Pan-American principles already approved had an ulterior importance for Argentina, was a declaration designated as Number XV. This was the Declaration of Reciprocal Assistance and Cooperation for the Defense of the American Nations, in which the following postulates were agreed to:

> That any attempt on the part of a non-American State against the integrity or inviolability of the territory, the sovereignty or the political independence of an American State shall be considered as an act of aggression against the States which sign this Declaration.
>
> In case acts of aggression are committed or should there be reason to believe that an act of aggression is being prepared by a non-American nation against the integrity or inviolability of the territory, the sovereignty or the political independence of an American nation, the nations signatory to the present declaration will consult among themselves in order to agree

upon the measure it may be advisable to take.

All the signatory nations, or two or more of them, according to circumstances, shall proceed to negotiate the necessary complementary agreement so as to organize cooperation for defense and the assistance that they shall lend each other in the event of aggressions such as those referred to in this Declaration.

The document was subscribed with a single reservation from Colombia, which voted *ad referendum* to its government as well as in accordance with the constitutional norms of the country. Argentina adhered without reservations.

The final paragraph of the cited text introduced a fundamental innovation, that of authorizing bilateral agreements as a means of completing the Pan-American system, although some detected in the abandonment of unanimity a symptom of slackness in Pan-Americanism. The truth is that this paragraph made it possible for the United States to conclude agreements with Latin American countries, by means of which she obtained the necessary bases for her armed forces in return for loans for arms and economic and financial aid. With the declaration voted in Havana, the "legal staging" for Lend-Lease was given. It would be on the basis of these bilateral agreements that the transforming program of Lend-Lease would make its effects felt in Latin America.

Spykman believes that on account of the great inequality between the contracting parties, the bilateral character of said agreements did not succeed in concealing their evident unilateralism. However, the transcendence of this policy would be shown not only in the strictly military field, but also in the economic evolution of the Latin American countries.

ECONOMIC MEASURES

In the face of the economic consequences of the war—the American countries aiming at regional undertakings and Argentina taking initiative—the regional economic conference of the River Plate met in Montevideo at the end of January 1941. Delegates from our country, Bolivia, Brazil, Paraguay, and Uruguay were present, and representatives from Peru, Chile, and the United States were not lacking. The general purpose of the meeting was to promote the development of regional trade among the participants in compensation for the considerable losses occasioned by the interruption of their trade with Europe on account of the war. Above all, it was sought to form an economic bloc whose members would trade freely among themselves.

A total of nine conventions and seventeen resolutions was adopted. Among them were included proposals for a regional system of highways and pipelines and of uniform transportation legislation. Although, on the other hand, a permanent office was established in Buenos Aires to direct the regional economic relations, an Argentine proposal for a customs union did not prosper.

Once this important meeting was over, Argentina concluded commercial treaties with almost all the nations of the continent. Those signed with Bolivia provided for the construction of railroads, roads, and pipelines; the agreements with Chile regulated the exchange of copper and nitrates from Chile for meat, cereals, and Argentine scrap iron; with Brazil, Argentina agreed not to compete in new industries and to gradually lower the tariffs as well as to exchange more wheat and industrial products for Brazilian coffee and textiles. The preamble of the treaty with Brazil sought to "establish a free trade regime that might permit the realization of a customs union between the Argentine Republic and the United States of Brazil, open to the adherence of the neighboring countries." Pacts with Peru and Colombia provided for the interchange of wheat for petroleum. Campbell estimates that 40 per cent of all the inter-South American trade was carried out with Argentina, and that its leadership was evident in the movement toward a regional economic bloc. As a result, Brazil, in order not to be outstripped during this frenzy, hastened to sign treaties with many of her neighbors. Almost all the countries were then sharing the Argentine watchwords of "neutrality" and "solidarity," but the entrance of the war into the hemisphere after Pearl Harbor broke up this panorama of coincidences. The pro-Ally bias shown by Uruguay cooled her relations with Argentina, while Brazil adopted a position of solidarity with the United States. With the passage of time, the Argentine sponsorship of an economic bloc began to appear as a movement against the United States, which precipitated its breakdown.

During the Havana conference of 1940 our delegation posed to the United States the increasing difficulties for our international trade created by the war and offered to sell to the United States our surplus of linen, leather, and meat. The North Americans judged that this was a possible base in order to reopen negotiations. After studying the problem, the Department of State advised the signing of an agreement that would, without doubt, alleviate the situation of Argentina without arousing distrust in the United States. On October 14, 1941, a commercial agreement between Argentina and the United States was signed, effective until November 14, 1944. Hull emphasizes that this was the first commercial agreement negotiated between the two countries in ninety years.

By virtue of this treaty, North American tariffs were reduced on 69 per cent of the imports from Argentina (including canned meat), and it was guaranteed that existing customs duties would not be increased and that new ones would not be imposed. Argentina reduced tariffs on only 18 per cent of her imports from the United States (among them automobiles and refrigerators) and promised not to increase existing tariffs on 12 per cent. The Argentine government maintained its quotas and its exchange control, but it obligated itself not to exercise them with prejudice to the United States, except in favor of Great Britain and the countries of the sterling area, as well as in favor of its neighbors and Peru.

AFTER PEARL HARBOR

Although Ortiz continued the Argentine neutralist tradition, his foreign policy revealed a certain flexibility in its adaptation to world events and to the inter-American commitments. Therefore, his withdrawal from office on account of illness, along with his being replaced in the executive functions by Vice President Castillo in July 1940, had visible repercussions in our international conduct. This evolution cannot be deduced from Castillo's first cabinet, formed immediately after the crisis of El Palomar with figures of openly pro-Ally tendencies such as Roca and Pinedo. But soon, in 1941, both ministers would be replaced by Enrique Ruiz Guiñazú and Carlos Alberto Acevedo. Ruiz Guiñazú, above all, coupled his limited international experience with a certain enthusiasm for the Hispanist version of Fascism. These circumstances perhaps accounted for his conviction that Madrid was the capital of the West and for his disdain of the culture and the war potentiality of the United States.

The policy of recalcitrant neutrality undertaken by Castillo and his foreign minister stemmed from various motivations. The international panorama was then favorable to the Axis powers, and to confront them would have brought exposure to a series of reprisals which, as Whitaker notes sharply, were not likely to come from the United Nations. Also, it was a matter of rolling along on the easy path of anti-Yankee phobia, which in Argentina always pays good dividends. This policy coincided with the virulent nationalism of the young personnel of the Right, of appreciable sectors of the middle class and of the army wherein the Conservative government was seeking support. Neutrality also had its plausible economic explanation, since it permitted Argentina to keep her traditional clients and also to acquire other new ones. In this Sumner Welles notes that for the Argentine people neutrality was equivalent to prosperity.

The war reached America December 7, 1941, when the Japanese attacked by surprise various American bases in the Pacific. The first Argentine reaction was the December 9 decree, Number 108,040. Its considerations specially corresponded to Declaration XV of the Havana meeting, to which the Argentine Republic adhered along with other American countries, in dealing with extracontinental aggression against the sovereignty of one of the American states and the violation of its territory. The dispositive part of the decree stated:

Article 1: The position of the Argentine Republic, in the present international conflict, will be guided in regard to the United States by the Pan-American agreements contracted on solidarity, mutual assistance and defense cooperations.

Article 2: In consequence, the Argentine Republic does not consider the United States of America in the position of a belligerent country in this conflict.

Article 3: The dispositions of the decree on neutrality dictated in the agreement of the ministers of September 4, 1939, are hereby extended to the present state of war only with respect to Great Britain and Japan.

Article 4: The Argentine Republic, in due time, and in accordance with the procedure provided by Declaration XV of the Havana meeting, previously cited, will proceed to negotiate the necessary complementary agreements.

In the face of the Japanese aggression, Chile and the United States proposed the convocation of the Third Meeting of the Foreign Ministers, with Rio de Janeiro selected as the meeting place. The conference took place between January 15 and 29. The Argentine delegation, headed by Ruiz Guiñazú, also included Eduardo Labougle, Luis E. Podestá Costa, Raúl Prebisch, Carlos L. Torriani, Ovidio V. Schiopetto, Enrique Ruiz Guiñazú, Jr., and Mario Octavio Amadeo.

The objectives sought by the United States from the conference had already been formulated by Roosevelt: first, to persuade all the American governments of the urgent necessity to break diplomatic relations and all commercial interchange with the Axis, in order to put an end to espionage and subversion in this hemisphere; second, to seek a basis for agreement on measures of military and naval cooperation necessary for the security of the American republics, as well as measures of indispensable collaboration, so that the countries of America could support the economic tension resulting from the war.

In this critical hour the Argentine government did not perceive the transcendental changes already at work in the world sphere. On the contrary, it persisted in the sophistries of its inveterate policy of neutrality. The war was arriving suddenly in America, and now was the propitious moment to demonstrate the solidarity of the links uniting all the countries of the hemisphere. For our country particularly it was the last occasion to attach herself to a current which was going to triumph and which, otherwise, would leave us behind in the race. But Argentina intended to construct a regional bloc in the hemisphere— with a double purpose: to bring the other countries to separatism and to exercise over them her leadership.

In those days there was much talk of the reconstruction of the ABC, and it was surmised that Argentina, Brazil and Chile were going to appear once again as a single bloc. The initiative did not prosper, however, because our neighbors did not want to isolate themselves from the rest of America. There was also an attempt to intercept various foreign ministers traveling through Buenos Aires on their way to Rio de Janeiro, with the hope of increasing the bloc with which to oppose the United States in the forthcoming meeting. On these grounds the Uruguayan foreign minister was invited, but he made known that he would not attend until after the Rio conference. However, the foreign ministers of Bolivia, Chile, Peru, and Paraguay were in our capital, and the attempts at dispersion were exercised on them. Thus, on January 7, during a luncheon in honor of his colleagues, Ruiz Guiñazú promoted such concepts as the "brotherhood of the Southern republics," "keeping America for peace," and "regional harmony in the economic sphere for the neighboring countries." To his host the Chilean foreign minister replied that "in America there are no distinctions between North, Central, and South. There is but one brotherhood—that of all the American peoples." The visiting ministers were to continue their trip in the company of the Argentine chancellor; but it did not materialize, for the Chilean advanced the date of his departure. This left only those of Peru and Paraguay, who also departed. Hence, in view of their failure to influence the neighboring nations, the Argentine representation, without its guests, undertook the trip by air some days later.

Once the Rio conference was inaugurated, Colombia, Mexico, and Venezuela presented to the Political Commission a project of rupture with the Axis, stated in these terms:

1. The American Republics declare that they consider the acts of aggression against one of the American Republics as acts of aggression against all of them, and as an immediate threat to the liberty and independence of the Western Hemisphere.

2. The American Republics confirm their complete solidarity and their determination to cooperate closely for their mutual protection until the present threat has completely disappeared.

3. In consequence, the American Republics manifest that in virtue of their solidarity, and for the purpose of preserving and protecting their integrity, none of them can continue maintaining political, commercial, or financial relations with the Governments of Germany, Italy, and Japan; at the same time, they declare that in full exercise of their sovereignty, they will take, individually or collectively, the measures corresponding to the defense of the New World which they consider practical and convenient in each case.

4. The American Republics declare, finally, that before re-newing their political, commercial, and financial relations with the aggressor powers, they will consider matters among themselves, so that their resolution may have a collective and solid character.

The Argentine delegation opposed this text and, in return, outlined another according to which "each American country will agree with the United States as to the form whereby it will extend such assistance in the concluding of the bilateral or mul-tilateral agreements necessary for the defense of the continent." This proposal was, of course, rejected, and after a week of nego-tiations the Argentine foreign minister agreed to subscribe to this version:

1. The American Republics reaffirm their declaration wherein they consider every act of aggression on the part of a non-American State as an act of aggression against all of them, since said act constitutes an act against the liberty and independence of America.

2. The American Republics reaffirm their complete solidarity and determination to cooperate in their mutual protection until the effects of the aggression against the continent shall have completely disappeared.

3. The American Republics consequently declare that in exer-cise of their sovereignty, and in conformity with their consti-tutional institutions and powers, provided that the latter agree, they cannot continue their diplomatic relations with Japan, Germany, and Italy, since Japan has effected attack and the other powers have declared war against a country of this continent.

4. The American Republics declare, finally, that before rees-tablishing relations, to which the above paragraph refers, they will consult among themselves, so that their decision can be collective and unanimous.

But the agreement reached on the basis of this formula was

ephemeral because President Castillo had hardly learned of it when, disavowing his own foreign minister, he manifested to the North American ambassador in Buenos Aires that he would not accept it. Hours later, the same Ruiz Guiñazú had to confess it in the meeting place of the conference. In the face of the unexpected objections from the Argentine chief executive to the project of resolution drafted by his minister of foreign affairs, the negotiations had to be renewed. Our delegation had no success with an attempt to replace the phrase of Article 3, "cannot continue their relations," by another very similar phrase that would have weakened its sense, "can discontinue their relations."

Some delegates wanted to sign the original version, leaving Chile and Argentina to follow a different path. But the majority, and above all Sumner Welles, decided to preserve at all costs the American unity and, thus, the following definitive form of recommendation was approved:

1. The American Republics reaffirm their declaration to consider any act of aggression on the part of a non-American State against one of them as an act of aggression against all of them, constituting as it does an immediate threat to the liberty and independence of America.

2. The American Republics reaffirm their complete solidarity and their determination to cooperate jointly for their mutual protection until the effects of the present aggression against the continent have disappeared.

3. The American Republics, in accordance with the procedures established by their own laws and in conformity with the position and circumstances obtaining in each country in the existing continental conflict, recommend the breaking of their diplomatic relations with Japan, Germany, and Italy, since the first-mentioned State attacked and the other two declared war on an American country.

4. Finally, the American Republics declare that, prior to the reestablishment of the relations referred to in the preceding

paragraph, they will consult among themselves in order that their action may have a solidary character.

A high price had been paid for the unanimity, for the concessions to the Argentine government stripped a great amount of force from the conference results. In fact, in order to obtain the support of all the countries, the resolution on rupturing diplomatic relations necessarily had to be transformed into a mere recommendation, whose third paragraph was nothing but a clause conditioned to reasons of opportunity to be judged by each country.

On being informed of the definitive text, Hull harshly rebuked Undersecretary Welles, and this split in the Department of State could not be healed, not even by President Roosevelt himself. It later provoked the withdrawal of Welles. For Hull the ambiguity of the solution reached would permit Argentina to easily elude her hemispheric obligations—an opinion soon to be confirmed by the facts. Welles, on the other hand, maintained that the compromise policy tolerated by him avoided greater evils for the Allied cause. His resignation left open the path to the hard and intransigent attitude of Hull, which characterized North American policy toward Argentina throughout the time it was under his direction.

But Argentina also paid dearly for its obstinacy in Rio. If not immediately, at least, the consequences were not slow to manifest themselves. The first reaction was the breakdown of the Lapez-Sueyro military-naval mission from Argentina, which was negotiating in the United States for the acquisition of armaments under the Lend-Lease system. Moreover, Argentina's isolation gave rise to a chilling climate that cast a pall over the existing attempts to project regional agreements with the neighboring countries dealing with economic and customs matters. The progress of these efforts might have been interpreted at that moment as a separatist manuever in hemispheric politics.

Finally, in stirring up an anti-Yankeeism—comprehensible decades before, but entirely anachronistic in 1942—Argentina began her bitter confrontation with the United States, that is, with the power already appearing as the principal victor in the war, at least to the eyes of halfway lucid observers. Among the latter, certainly, one did not find the Argentine government team.

If for Welles the rupture of relations with the Axis constituted the principal objective of the conference, and if for Argentina the adoption of a position independent from the United States was the essential question—the great part of the Latin American delegates were fundamentally interested in economic problems. By the end of 1941 the United States was the principal market and the principal source of supply for the American countries. The latter depended more than ever on the former country for the solution of their economic problems. In this respect they seemed eager to receive some commitment that not only essential imports be guaranteed, but also the program of industrial reactivation, which the United States was defending for the rest of the continent. There is no possible doubt that the North American economic influence, expanded because of the war by the disappearance of the European market, was the decisive factor on which that country relied in order to gain the submission of its no longer wayward neighbors to the suggestions of the Rio de Janeiro conference.

In his opening speech Welles promised that his country would extend for the needs of the American republics a consideration equal to and in proportion with the necessities of the United States. In agreement with the preamble, the majority of the resolutions adopted by the conference, based in great part on the program presented by the North American delegation, were directed toward the "economic mobilization" of the hemisphere. Such resolutions sought to promote the increase of the production of strategic materials, essential for the conduct of the war

(Resolution II). In support of this the conference adopted measures directed toward the improvement of the means of transportation, toward the coordination of navigation services (Resolution IV), and toward the simplification of the problems of exchange (Resolution XV). On her part, the United States undertook the support of the internal economies of the American countries and committed herself to preventing a rise in the price of production materials (Resolution III). Also she obligated herself to invest capital in the American republics (Resolution XI) and to collaborate in the economic improvement of the soil and the subsoil (Resolution XVI). The countries that had heretofore failed to do so were to establish special commissions for the purpose of drawing up the necessary plans for economic mobilization. The Inter-American Financial and Economic Advisory Committee—created in the first consultation meeting of the American Foreign Ministers at Panama—was to be in charge of coordinating the plans.

CONTRADICTIONS OF NEUTRALISM

Castillo and his Foreign Minister Ruiz Guiñazú resorted to all kinds of arguments in defense of their peculiar international attitude. And their anxiety to explain everything involved them in more than a few contradictions.

Insofar as possible, they tried to underrate the importance of the consultation meetings held by American foreign ministers and to reduce them to a simple exchange of ideas and opinions whose results would be lyric documents deprived of any obligatory force. Thus, Ruiz Guiñazú, in his book *La política Argentina y el futuro de América*, written in order to justify the part that befell him, maintains that Declaration XV of Havana (1940) "has never had parliamentary ratification in our country." Nevertheless, Decree 108,040, issued by Castillo December 9, 1941, and countersigned by Ruiz Guiñazú himself, discounts his full force because it says that "Whereas to this effect it is especially appropriate to make mention of Declaration XV of the Havana meeting, to which the Argentine Republic along with the other American countries subscribed in dealing with an extracontinental aggression against the sovereignty of one of the States and the violation of its territory." And he adds in the dispositive part of Article 4 quoted above.

Another habitual recourse on the part of the President, as well as that of the foreign minister, consisted in manifesting to the outside world a good will limited by the faculties of the Argentine Congress, while on the domestic level they always turned deaf ears toward the claims of Congress by virtue of the constitutional attributions of the chief executive. The most evident case was that of the Argentine delegation's scruples at Rio about signing agreements, namely, the rupture of relations, which could bring us to a state of belligerency without the previous authorization of our Congress.

When, however, the Chamber of Deputies in September 1942 moved to ratify the instruments in the Rio conference and to require the consequent break in relations, this punctilious executive branch reminded the Chamber dryly that the management of foreign relations was its sole attribute, and that the Rio documents had been sent to Congress only for informative purposes. Similar inconsistency could be observed in the management of the armaments in connection with the credits sought from the North American government.

According to Argentine leaders, the break in relations with the Axis, as established at Rio, signified a belligerent posture which, obviously enough, could not be adopted without the previous authorization of Congress; furthermore, it was at the moment not appropriate for the nation in view of the risks that were involved. But, the previously mentioned Decree 108,040 of 1941, in declaring nonbelligerent one of the great powers intervening in the struggle, already signified for our country a reciprocally belligerent attitude with respect to the opposed powers. It can also be added that this decree was dictated without the previous authorization of Congress. Finally, in the Rio conference, the Argentine foreign minister claimed that the unexpected Japanese attack on Pearl Harbor and other Pacific bases did not constitute a typical continental aggression since it involved Asiatic possessions of the United States. Thus, even in 1944, Ruiz Guiñazú in his book recalled: "This extracontinental fact, with an exclusively Asiatic origin. . . ."

But the same Decree 108,040 recognized two days after the Japanese attack that it was a question of "an extracontinental aggression on the sovereignty of one of the American states and the violation of one of its territories."

4: ARMS AND PROGRESS

THE SPEARS AND CHRISTIAN MISSIONS

When in May 1940 the German tanks broke through the frontier in order to cross the Forest of Ardennes, the fate of France and Belgium was indeed sealed, as well as that of the English expeditionary force. That "phalanx of fire and steel" brought down not only the European balance of power, but also the first line of defense for America. The United States felt herself threatened. There remained no other barrier than that of the Atlantic, and this could be crossed.

North American public opinion understood the necessity of placing the continent in a state of alert, and the government issued a new policy of Atlantic defense. It tried to unite the forces of the American nations in order to guarantee hemispheric protection. The United States feared that the Reich, ally of Spain, would sneak along the African coast toward Dakar and from there—only 1,845 miles from the Brazilian salient of Cape San Rocque—would reach and surprise the heart of a South America that was disarmed.

All this explains the Latin American search for collaboration toward the common defense of the continent, as well as the construction and utilization of bases in South America. Only thus can be understood the sustained attention that the United States paid to Africa. The same can be said for the vigilance with which the United States followed every new development in the Azores, in the Canaries, and in the Cape Verde Islands— in all that archipelago, which from the coast of Europe and

73

of Africa dominates the routes toward America. This danger would shortly disappear with the American expedition to Africa (October 1942).

On May 20, 1940, from Washington, Ambassador Espil informed the Argentine Foreign Ministry that the defensive base of the United States was turning to the question of defense for the continent. He presumed that the North American government would want to explore the Argentine position on the coordination of a defense plan in the event of an attack on any part of the hemisphere, and he counseled that all the possibilities be considered with prudence.

Effectively, on May 24, the Embassy of the United States delivered to our Foreign Ministry a memorandum in which it expressed the concern of its government in the critical aspect the war had assumed, as well as in its interest that all the American republics might establish secret communications for the purpose of coordinating their forces should any act of aggression be carried out. It was added that this suggestion:

> did not imply any military alliance, any military or naval commitment . . . this suggestion only implies that the government of the United States believes the world situation has become more and more dangerous, and that it therefore appears prudent on the part of the American republics to determine the role each one would be able to play in case they were obliged to resist aggression against the peace of the New World, avoiding thereby duplication of their forces in the event of such emergency.

Another memorandum dated May 31 clarified that the defensive measures in charge of our country

> would be especially limited to the naval forces the Argentine government would be able to utilize, for the protection of its own coast and perhaps the Uruguayan coast, against a foreign aggression.

Captain William O. Spears was charged with officially consulting our navy about some questions of interest to the navy of his country. An order from Minister León Scasso designated Captains Francisco Clarissa and Francisco Renta—the latter being second chief of the general staff—to carry out discussions with Spears. On June 10 these two, together with Pablo Santos Muñoz, representing the Foreign Ministry, engaged in the first consultation with the North American envoy, who had limited himself to the following questions: whether the Argentine government would be disposed to cooperate militarily with the American countries, specifically with the United States, in the case of an aggression against the continent by extracontinental countries. In the case of an affirmative answer, whether the Argentine government would put together defense plans and indicate the naval and aviation bases required to execute them; and in the latter case, what needs would Argentina have and what aid could she supply.

It was especially important to the United States envoy to learn whether the Argentine Government would permit use of her waters, ports, as well as naval and air bases to oppose a threat to neighboring countries such as Uruguay and Brazil. The Argentine representatives did not reply immediately. Hours later the marine minister ordered the general staff to have Renta answer Spears to the effect that "the Argentine navy does not have the facilities to answer the questions formulated. Although Argentina is grateful for the offer of aid, it is evident that she does not consider it necessary. It is felt that in the hypothetical case of an attack, the Argentine people would know how to defend themselves against any threat to their sovereignty."

But Spears held his ground by affirming that he had made the trip to coordinate plans with the Argentines. Renta replied that first of all the foreign ministers should hold a meeting. The North American's response indicated that such programming would only forestall the element of time.

On the heels of this exploratory criterion on defense coordination, the United States ambassador on June 17 presented the Foreign Ministry with a confidential memorandum, which inquired whether the Argentine government, in the case of an aggression against Uruguay, would lend aid and would cooperate with his country in order to resist that aggression. He asked also if the same attitude would be maintained in the case of aggression by a non-American state against any other American republic. And in the case that a base should be established on the Atlantic coast, which might threaten Argentina, would she desire aid from the United States, and could North American aid count on facilities in Argentine ports and aviation fields? In order to make plans accordingly, discussions were arranged within a short space of time between the general naval staffs of both countries.

The Foreign Ministry sought the advice of the minister of war and minister of navy as to the content of the memorandum. The first opinion, signed by General Márquez—upon immediately considering grave any aggression against Uruguay and Brazil, before which the country could not remain indifferent—accepted the propositions of the document. On the contrary, after reviewing the territorial growth of the United States and referring to the "politics of the dollar," the naval minister, Scasso, answered negatively to the questionnaire; he opposed particularly the reference to collaboration of elements and bases, and believed that any attempt at negotiation should be abandoned.

For his part, Argentine Minister of Foreign Relations Cantilo replied June 28 to the North American ambassador that

> Argentina has at no time needed a special pact in order to come to the defense of an American country unjustly attacked. And, without a doubt, if another American republic whose closeness to Argentina made feasible the aid, and if the country should request it, the Congress would authorize it. If

Argentina were the object of an aggression, then she would be relying on the aid that other American republics might offer.

True inter-American collaboration ought to be permanent and should embrace the commerical and cultural fields; these republics will then progress and will be able to reserve for national defense such adequate sums that no world power would dare to attempt the risk involved in any aggression on the American continent.

He concludes with an affirmation that if, unfortunately, a dangerous situation should develop, it would be investigated not only with the United States, but also with the other American governments.

After the Havana Conference (1940), the efforts on the part of the North American high command were renewed. Lieutenant Colonel R. L. Christian, after talks with superior officials of Paraguay and Uruguay, established himself for the same purpose in Buenos Aires. On September 25 Foreign Minister Roca informed Chargé d'affaires Tuck that the ministers of war and navy were agreeable to talk with Lieutenant Colonel Christian. The latter was then joined by the naval attaché, Brereton, in accordance with the proposal of the North American government.

At the beginning of these discussions, Christian referred to the preparation for common defense of the continent in the case of aggression on the part of a non-American power against a Central American or South American state. He made manifest that only an exchange of ideas was sought between professionals, with no implication of pacts for which commitment was impossible—since such commitment was a question for the governments. He asked for the greatest frankness in the statements and clarified that in no way was there any intention of seizing bases or forcing any country to cede them.

The chief of the general staff of the Argentine navy, Vice

Admiral Julián Fablet, summed up the North American efforts in the following manner:

Having studied the questions from Captain Spears and those obtained from Lieutenant Colonel Christian, one reaches the conclusion they have again insisted on a decision from our country, although in moderate form. Our position is in no way comfortable; in the North, Brazil is reaching an understanding with the United States, acquiring credits and arming itself; in the West, Chile, in spite of its poverty, goes along acquiring material of war and has obtained a credit to construct a dry dock for ships of 45,000 tons.

Meanwhile, everything in our country is stagnating. A danger lies in the increase in arms in Brazil and in Chile, and in the certainty that they will be provisioned in case of war against our country. These countries can be the executors in order to obtain for the United States control of the coastline, which she needs in event of an obstruction of the Panama Canal.

The American commissioner asks for collaboration only in the case of an armed attack of a non-American country against Central and South American nations. Under this point of view, it is possible to maintain friendly relations with the United States. We would construct the naval bases on the South Coast and employ technicians and capital from North America, if necessary, as well as manufacturing munitions, powder, explosives, and so on. Thus, without North American control, collaboration would be limited only to repairs and supplies for American units. With this, the country abandons neutrality, but the dilemma consists in whether we will be able to maintain the same and with it our territorial integrity.

For his part, the delegate of the Argentine navy, who had carried out the negotiations with Lieutenant Colonel Christian, informed his superiors that "perhaps we have not satisfied their wishes fully, but this is due not to the lack of good disposition, but to the fact that many of the proposed themes exceed the limit of our instructions and even of the ministry itself, because they are concerned with matters of international policy."

The Argentine government's answer to the proposals from Spears and Christian was qualified by North American authorities as "general and evasive responses." The latter part of these first dealings seems to indicate a lack of interest on the part of the Argentine government on behalf of hemispheric security. This also explains the reticent and dilatory attitude toward North American attempts at military cooperation.

THE LEND-LEASE ACT

In the months of November and December 1940, Foreign Minister Roca informed Ambassador Armour that Argentina would be disposed to renew the official talks between commissioners from the two countries "as soon as the military requirements of her government become more clearly established." Under reference were two proposals of law, at that moment under consideration in Congress, which were later approved April 22, and September 9, 1941, as Numbers 12,672 and 12,690. These laws authorized the employment of funds for the acquisition of material for the Argentine army and navy—amounting to 646,474,545 pesos for the army, and 712,000,000 pesos for the navy. According to the prevailing exchange rate (about 384.34 pesos for $100) they represented 191 and 210 million dollars respectively.

On March 11, 1941, North America voted the Lend-Lease Act, and with it the United States assumed a state of semi-belligerency, which would soon end at Pearl Harbor with her entrance into the war. The law authorized the President when he considered it of interest for the national defense to sell, barter, transfer, lease, or lend every kind of article for the protection of the government of any country whose defense the President considers vital for the United States. The United States thereby became the arsenal of democracy. With all due respect to her farsighted measures, she succeeded in sufficient time to adapt production to the necessities of war; otherwise, it would have been impossible. Hence United States action placed at the service of the allies some fifty billion dollars in arms, food, and services.

Independently, the Lend-Lease Act signified a revolutionary fact, inasmuch as the United States put into practice for the first time—and on a large scale—the "policy of the gift,"* which later she would repeat with so much success to defend and maintain her world leadership. The gifts are economic transferals without credits or loans from the country that receives them. Capital or goods may be given in conditions of extreme favor. These operations have a political end that is generally openly admitted, based on a scheme that massive aid is preferable to a plan of defense of equivalent cost—if not greater cost or to war itself. All this does not prevent certain advantages from accruing to the donor country, since the economic activation of the country receiving aid increases exchange and has the effect of returning benefits to the country that undertook the aid.

The policy of Lend-Lease, of practically giving away armaments, had unforeseen consequences in Latin America. The countries that benefited obtained the most modern equipment for their armed forces, which factor drastically altered the military equilibrium in this part of the continent. Up to the time of war, Argentine supremacy was perceptible in the regional military terrain. In March 1938 a note from Ritter, Hitler's ambassador in Rio, informed the Wilhelmstrasse of the Brazilian concern because

> The only potential adversary of Brazil in the military field is Argentina. But at present, and for a long time to date, Brazil from the military point of view has found herself in a situation of inferiority with respect to Argentina.
>
> The nucleus of Brazil's military power, which is also that of its industrial power, is now in the states of the center: Sao

* The authors use the English word *gift*.

Paulo, Rio de Janeiro, and Minas Gerais. But this center of power has practically no strategic railroad connections with the states of the South. On account of the naval superiority of Argentina, the military communications with the states of the South, by sea, would in case of a conflict be controlled by Argentina.

The delivery of arms revived the pure nationalism of the South American countries and renewed their ancient rivalries. During this period Argentina in the final analysis tried to reconcile two irreducible extremes: on the one side, to maintain itself neutral; on the other, to prevent an increasing military inferiority in the face of the economic and military strengthening of the neighboring countries, thanks to the North American aid under Lend-Lease.

Shortly after the law was approved, Espil, in a confidential note to the foreign minister, pointed out the faculties granted to President Roosevelt by this new legal instrument: "To designate any country whose defense he may consider vital to the United States, which is so broad a condition that it does not exclude any or all of the American countries, be they or not objects of actual aggression."

He also gave notice that, according to the declaration of the army chief of staff, General Marshall, negotiations were under way with various governments, among them Brazil, to supply them with material of war under the authorizations of Lend-Lease.

Ambassador Espil was called to the Department of State on April 29 by Undersecretary Welles who informed him that—in accordance with the exploratory missions his government had sent to the military and naval authorities of the South American countries, seeking to coordinate defense measures for the continent—various American governments were already accumulating credits to acquire material of war. Welles said that President Roosevelt had decided to make use of the faculties conferred on him by the Lend-Lease Act, and thus to provide

material to the countries of the continent requiring it. Espil
reported:

> In the case of Argentina, in spite of the cordiality shown
> during the exploratory discussions, the Argentine authorities
> had avoided any intelligence on defense coordination. In spite
> of all this, the plan of estimates for the materials of war that
> the United States was disposed to facilitate to the American
> countries had provided for and budgeted the sum of 21 mil-
> lion dollars for the needs of the navy—if the latter appeared
> interested in acquiring this material and would decide to
> negotiate in this respect. Should the offer be accepted, it
> would be possible later on to agree about the form of pay-
> ment for this material. For example, we [Argentina] could
> deliver certain strategic materials such as tungsten.

In accordance with this offer, on July 30, 1941, Ambassador
Armour presented the Foreign Ministry with a confidential
memorandum in which he reported that the government of
the United States had decided to apportion in the next few
years, through the American republics, military and naval material of an approximate value of 400 million dollars. It was
further reported that in the present circumstances the only possibility for the Argentine government to obtain delivery of naval
and military material in the near future was that provided under
the Lend-Lease Act. He closed the memorandum with the information that Undersecretary of State Welles had understood that
the Argentine government was disposed to renew the talks the
general staffs had begun in Buenos Aires during the visits of
Captain Spears and Lieutenant Colonel Christian. He would
suggest, then, that there be designated a naval-military commission, which would visit the United States at an early date
with the authority not only to continue the conversations begun
in Buenos Aires the year before, but also to present the needs
of the Argentine government with respect to naval and military
equipment.

THE LAPEZ-SUEYRO MISSION

To deal with the North American proposal, the Ministerial Cabinet was called into session August 13, with Castillo presiding. Here, Ruiz Guiñazú analyzed the arms laws recently passed by the Argentine Congress, in order to relate them to the acquisition of war materials in the United States. According to his opinion, if the armaments were under the system of the Lend-Lease Act, then Argentina was beginning de facto and de jure the application of continental defense, since under this condition they were authorized by the government of the United States. The exposition rendered by the foreign minister tended to reveal that in this way "Argentina was entering the orbit of the so-called benefits that the United States was trying to dispense to the 'democracies,' which logically placed [the country] under the military control of the United States."

In spite of Ruiz Guiñazú's reservations, it was agreed to designate a naval-military commission—which would include the Argentine ambassador in Washington—that would apply itself to the acquisition of armaments.

Ruiz Guiñazú's expression in the Cabinet, referring to the fact that Argentina with the purchase of armaments was placing herself de facto and de jure under the North American military control, was promptly clarified. Five days later, August 18, Armour interviewed Undersecretary Gache, to whom he pointed out that the sale of weapons under the Lend-Lease system might be mistakenly interpreted as a "subordination of these sales and these facilities to plans of continental defense that the Government of the United States has wished to consider with the Argentine Government."*

On September 4 a meeting in the Foreign Ministry was attended by Ruiz Guiñazú; Admiral Fincate, minister of navy;

* The quotation is translated from the authors' citation of Undersecretary Gache's memorandum.

and General Casinelli, inspector general of the army. At this meeting Admiral Fincate affirmed that the navy would not subscribe to the armaments agreement if thereby it should be necessary to make the least concession that might injure Argentine sovereignty. He cited in support of his thesis the presence of North American observers in Brazilian ports. Ruiz Guiñazú immediately tried to confirm North American meddling. The following day he cabled the Argentine ambassadors in Rio and in Washington to ask that they report whether, as a consequence of the facilities granted by the government of the United States under the Lend-Lease system, there had been reached any form of intervention or control in the countries of America, especially in Brazil; if officers of the United States had been detailed to duty there; and whether they discharged functions on the military and naval bases.

The replies of the officials consulted, however, clouded the matter. Labougle, ambassador in Rio, spoke of the North American naval attaché, "who is a rear admiral, has at his disposition five aides, an airplane with a pilot and a crew of six persons, and that for the construction of bases at Belem, where 5,000 workers are employed, 25 technicians have arrived." Espil, on his part, answered:

> There are no serious reasons to suppose that the United States may exercise, or may try to exercise, any form of intervention or control in the countries of America under pretext of the facilities that it grants according to the plan of continental defense. With regard to the North American chiefs and officers recently detailed in the countries of Latin America, it is undeniable that an active movement in this sense exists, but it would be risky to affirm that they discharge functions in the naval and the military bases.

Meanwhile, General Tonazzi, minister of war, had returned from Brazil where he had been invited together with the chief of the general staff, General Juan Pierrestegui, on the occasion of the national holiday of that country. They returned impressed by the preparation of the Brazilian troops and in a special way by the modern material the latter possessed. In fact, on occasion of the September 7 parade, the Brazilian army exhibited tanks, hundreds of trucks, and heavy artillery, all new and provided by North American aid. The report given by General Tonazzi on that occasion emphasized the danger of a short-term Argentine military inferiority, should the country continue on the margin of the benefits of Lend-Lease. The report stimulated, without any doubt, the steps undertaken for the purchase of armaments.

Ruiz Guiñazú, in accordance with suggestions from the military ministers, asked for the agenda to be considered in the discussions between the naval and military chiefs from Argentina and the United States. Armour informed the foreign minister that according to instructions received, he was submitting for consideration this proposed agenda:

> Effort should be made to reach an agreement with respect to the action each of the countries would realize in the following circumstances: (a) in event Argentina and the United States were associated in a war against the enemy; (b) in event one country would remain nonbelligerent while the other would enter the war.

Regarding the first alternative, it would be necessary to (1) decide on the best methods of cooperation between the armed forces of Argentina and the United States; (2) coordinate plans of cooperation; (3) reach agreements regarding the nature and methods of military cooperation between both nations that would include the assignment of zones of responsibility, the principal lines of military strategy to be adopted by both countries, as well as the strength of the armed forces to be provided by each nation. Besides, it would be necessary to determine plans of adequate command, regarding both the unity of command in the terrain of activities and the supreme military control in the case of joint operations, either technical or strategic.

The object of the second alternative would be to decide what action each country could undertake within the limits of its own policy for the defense of the hemisphere. This discussion would include a question referring to naval and aerial control, in order to protect legitimate commerce in the South Atlantic.

Obviously enough, the last paragraph clarifies the requirement, as clearly specified in the beginning, of the "convoy whose inclusion would later on break up the negotiations and place Argentina at the margin of the armament program of Lend-Lease."

On August 19, 1941, Decree 106,056—wherein allusion was made to the invitation extended by the North American government, to the agenda of themes to be treated in Washington (detailed in the personal note from Armour, September 29, cited above) and to the declarations of Lima and Havana on reciprocal assistance and defense cooperation—designated a naval-military commission headed by Rear Admiral Sabá H. Sueyro and Brigadier General Eduardo T. Lapez. The commission included the following naval personnel: Commanders Harold Cappus, Aureliano G. Lares, Carlos Garzoni, and Lieutenant Manuel N. Bianchi; and army personnel: Lieutenant Colonel Raúl Ruiz Díaz, Major Emilio Loza, and Captain Luis M. A. Terradas. In accordance with the decree, Ambassador Espil also became part of the commission "for all matters that may be of interest to the international policy of the country."

Before they arrived in Washington, Espil had an interview with officers of the Department of State and had indicated to them that perhaps his government might make use of the facilities and releases for the payment of armaments similar to those authorized for the other American countries. Up to this moment the negotiations had been carried out under the condition of purchase for cash. The request for facilities signified, without any doubt, a change in the negotiations. According to this new plan, another proposal for basic agreement was delivered to Espil. The first article determined that

> the United States of America proposes to transfer to the Argentine Republic, in accordance with the terms of this agreement, armaments and munitions of war up to an approximate value of 66 million dollars. The United States proposes to initiate the deliveries immediately and to continue them with the greatest possible rapidity during the first twelve months up to an approximate value of 15 million dollars for the use of the Argentine army and up to an approximate value of one million dollars for the use of the Argentine navy.

And it was established by virtue of the second article that

> the government of the United States agrees to accord to the government of the Argentine Republic a reduction of 45.45 per cent in the total cost of the materials that will be delivered in fulfillment of the stipulations of the present agreement.

Pearl Harbor

The conversations between the naval-military commission from Argentina and the North American officials had hardly begun when, in the early hours of Sunday, December 7, 1941, Japanese airplanes attacked and destroyed the Pacific Fleet of the United States in Pearl Harbor; this signified war. The Roosevelt government, two days later, invited the other American governments to join in the Third Meeting of the Foreign Ministers, which began in Rio de Janeiro January 15, 1942. There is no doubt, as noted previously, that the Argentine attitude at that meeting led to deterioration of the good relations maintained with the United States up to that moment. The delegation presided by Ruiz Guiñazú, in accordance with instructions from Castillo, refused to accept the initial proposal that obligated the American republics to an immediate rupture. Finally, facing the fear of losing unanimity, the United States accepted the formula that "recommended" (without making it obligatory) the breaking of diplomatic relations with the Axis, leaving to each country the decision as to whether and when it would break these relations.

The neutrality, which the Castillo government strove to maintain after the attack on Pearl Harbor, necessarily led the United States to utilize pressure in order to obtain Argentine acceptance. This policy of pressure left its impact, as was logical, in the negotiations on armaments under way in Washington. However —aside from the commission headed by Sueyro and Lapez— pressure had been applied previously when at the Rio conference itself Sumner Welles rejected a request from Ruiz Guiñazú for North American armaments. In fact, shortly after the beginning of the consultation meeting January 19, Acting Chancellor Rothe cabled Ruiz Guiñazú that, by direction from Castillo, he should concern himself with obtaining from the government of the United States facilities and support for the establishment of heavy industry in our country, particularly the industry engaged in the production of materials of defense, armaments, airplanes, munitions, and so forth. Ruiz Guiñazú replied to the Foreign Ministry that

> in conversation with the undersecretary of state, I have sustained that it is indispensable for our country to be able to count on the regular provision of materials of war, of equipment and raw materials, as well as on the development of heavy industry.*

To this request Welles replied that

* Ruiz Guiñazú, in La política argentina y el futuro de America (p. 182) denies having solicited arms, and refutes Welles who has stated the case in Time for Decision. Without doubt this cable from Ruiz Guiñazú himself proves the former North American undersecretary to be correct.

until the Argentine government had at least taken steps to comply with the terms of the resolution adopted the day before, had broken relations of every character with the Axis, and was acutally contributing what it could in defending the Western Hemisphere from Axis attacks, it was useless to enter into any conversation on this subject.

The consequences of the Argentine attitude at Rio de Janeiro began to make themselves felt also in Washington. Espil reported that as yet it was not possible to obtain from the North American authorities precise definitions on the problem of armaments; in continuation he said he had to admit that the "immediate perspectives are hardly encouraging." Days later in Buenos Aires, Armour had an interview with Acting Foreign Minister Rothe (Ruiz Guiñazú was at this moment visiting Chile). And to the apparent anticipation that the material of war necessary for defense would be received from the United States, the Ambassador replied that "he must of course realize the situation had changed materially since the Río conference," and that his country would supply, in the first place, nations which had broken relations with the Axis and which, thereby, had exposed themselves to the danger of an attack.

The denial of any other type of military assistance, as a coercive means to effect a change in the position of the Argentine government, received official consecration, when on February 4 Welles communicated with his ambassador:

I have consulted General Marshall and Admiral Stark. They will tomorrow inform Admiral Sueyro and General Lapez that inasmuch as the Argentine Government has determined to maintain at least for the time being a position which is tantamount to neutrality and inasmuch as all but one of the other American Republics have either declared war or broken relations with the Axis powers and have thereby incurred the dangers inherent in such action through their support of the United States, the military and naval matériel which can be spared by the United States can logically be allotted only to the latter American nations.

On February 9, after an incidental conversation, Welles officially notified Espil that although the "possibilities for providing armaments to the American countries would be considered without any purpose of discrimination" *de facto* situations could arise in which, by reason of insufficient material, "it might be necessary to give priority to those countries, which by reason of rupture of relations, might be in danger beyond those that had not exposed themselves and had continued in maintaining them [relations]."

In spite of the somber reports from Espil and the declarations from Armour himself, the greatest optimism prevailed throughout official Argentine circles. The Foreign Ministry was prepared to go even further, for on February 7 it ordered the ambassador in Washington that

in accordance with the recommendation by the ministers of war and navy, and with the approval and general agreement of the ministers, the ambassador will prepare and propose to this Ministry of Foreign Relations a new text for fundamental agreement in accordance with the Lend-Lease Act with the following bases:

1. The quotas of provisions will correspond in total to 200 million dollars for the army, 250 million dollars for the navy.

2. On the sum of the materials transferred, the Argentine government will pay 50 per cent of the value in six annual installments in accordance with the costs resulting from the awards. The other 50 per cent will be assumed by the government of the United States in compensation for the contribution the government is making to the other, in the form of facilities, for the acquisition of strategic materials in Argentina, and for the prejudices affecting the Argentine finance and economy on account of the state of war and the difficulties of her foreign commerce.

3. The transfers will be carried out in two parts in the years 1942 and 1943, and they will correspond to the lists of the new plan of armaments, which will complement that presented in 1941, and which is already insufficient in view of the change in the situation. This detailed and specific plan will be delivered to the ambassador through the intermediary of the naval-military delegation.

There were notable differences from the proposals sent from Washington by Espil before the Rio conference. Now they were asking for 450 million dollars instead of the 66 million agreed on in the original project: the delivery of the material in two years, instead of six; a discount of 50 per cent on the total sum of the operation, instead of the 45.45 per cent formerly established.

The communication from the Foreign Ministry continued:

It is not possible to limit oneself strictly to the quota of 66 million dollars assigned to our country by virtue of the Lend-Lease Act, passed when the circumstances were different from the present and when the obligations to be assumed in the Argentine zone of responsibility had not been spelled out. Therefore, it is convenient that the government of the United States appreciate the necessity of obtaining, if it is judged necessary, the inclusion of the increase which we need in an additional, or new, Lend-Lease law, whose sanction would be proposed to the legislative branch.

This strongly suggests the absolute conviction of the Argentine government as to the high strategic value obtained by the country—thanks to its position in the Rio conference. Only this conviction could carry it to the point of not fearing a change in Washington's attitude after the Argentine performance in that conference. On the contrary, the government displayed a confidence mixed with ingenuity in asking for increases in the delivery of arms, as well as new facilities, and even advised that

for it the United States Congress might vote an additional law
to the Lend-Lease Act. That same day, February 17, from the
North American side, in strong contrast with the communication from our Foreign Ministry, Welles requested of the chief
of naval operations, Admiral Stark, that the representatives of
the United States should sign no agreement with the Argentine
commission; he took equal precautions regarding the army. The
bad news from Espil was not expected: "Acting Secretary of
State Welles told me yesterday how much he feared that that
plan would not be in agreement with the basic defense necessities of the United States and her allies under the present circumstances, and that he did not believe that in the last instance
it would be recommended by the Navy Department."

The Convoy

On March 15, 1942, Admiral Sueyro, Espil, and Minister
García Arias met with Welles in the residence of the ambassador in Washington. The meeting was held at the request of
Welles himself. In the course of the conversation he pointed
out the difficulties the United States was encountering in providing armaments to the countries needing them without delay.
He stressed the urgent necessity of aid to Brazil, practically
involved in the war, and he then referred to the critical situation
of Chile with its extensive coastline almost undefended. Welles
emphasized to the others that the United States had just sent
to the latter some coastal artillery, and he also pointed out the
urgency of providing Peru and Ecuador with certain defense
elements. He qualified the Argentine policy of nonbelligerency
as somewhat negative in the present state of the conflict and
insisted on the necessity of establishing a "convoy" for the protection of inter-American commerce and of participation of the
Argentine navy therein, at least as far as the beginning of the

Brazilian coast. Admiral Sueyro replied that it was impossible, because his country's navy lacked elements for this function, and that the matter had been examined in a technical discussion which concluded that this collaboration was not viable. Welles, on his part, insisted that he desired any measure of active collaboration—however limited it may be on the part of the Argentine government—as something to modify in North American public opinion the predominant impression that the Argentine was maintaining itself withdrawn and indifferent to the conflict.

On the following day it was announced that the meetings between the Argentine commission and the North Americans would be postponed for one or two weeks in expectation of a counterproposal from the latter. The newly projected agenda would refer to a plan of cooperation between both navies, in event the United States continued in war with non-American enemies and the Argentine remained neutral, that is to say, the situation obtaining at that moment. It was established in the first place that in accordance with the offer of the Argentine government to consider the United States nonbelligerent, that government would give logistic aid to any North American naval force visiting its ports, anchorages, or bases. Furthermore, Argentina recognized the necessity to maintain uninterrupted the maritime communications between the United States and herself. For this purpose both governments would determine the respective areas in which their navies would be responsible for the tasks of convoy, corresponding to our navy the course from the south of Brazil to the Argentine ports and vice-versa. The proposal was completed by the North American agreement that in spite of Argentine nonbelligerence, it would immediately open negotiations in order to conclude a basic agreement regarding materials and facilities provided for the year 1942.

The maritime line of the Atlantic coast between Newfoundland and Rio de la Plata had the heaviest traffic in the world. Across it came ships transporting petroleum, iron, steel, cotton, sugar, coffee, bauxite, and meat from the sources of production to the most important Allied markets. The submarines were in effect maintaining target practice with these ships. The most practical means of protection was to require them to proceed in coastal convoys, but the convoys were useless without escort; hence, what the United States so urgently needed at this moment was precisely escort vessels.

The Argentine delegation replied that the North American proposal for convoy ". . . was a political question and, consequently, beyond the competence and authorization of this delegation for its consideration. It is regretted that this delegation stands incompetent to discuss the plan of cooperation." To this was added that even now it was corresponding with the political authorities of the two countries to discuss this matter. This obstacle of "assigning to the convention a political character alien to the attributions of the military-naval delegation"—which Ruiz Guiñazú himself hastened to reiterate to Espil—was not insurmountable, since Article 3 of Decree 106,056 established that said naval-military commission would be "integrated by the ambassador of the Republic in the United States, or the chief of that mission, for all the matters which may concern the international policy of the country." Also, the chancery itself, in a confidential communiqué of November 28, 1941, had instructed Espil that he should consult it in such case.

The Foreign Ministry maintained that the obligation for convoy created a situation of belligerency, which Argentina did not want and for which it was not prepared. The convoy, without a doubt, would be a definite step toward rupture if not toward war itself, since the use of Argentine war vessels for this purpose would inevitably lead to an armed conflict with the Axis. Argentina, in fulfillment of her military duty, could not tolerate visits or captures on the part of the Axis—being that her duty in such cases was to repel them by force.

On the North American side, it was argued that the torpedo-

ing of foreign vessels with products destined for Argentina signified a virtual blockade, which this country ought to impede; the
contrary would be to pretend that other nations should guarantee commercial traffic and normal supplies while the interested
state remained neutral. The United States considered that the
formulated proposal to our country—to protect maritime traffic
in its adjacent waters—was just and reasonable, since it meant
utilizing all the disposable forces for the protection of the North
Atlantic, and even the South Atlantic, including the vessels
destined for traffic with Argentina. It was therefore concluded
that the least the latter could do was to protect these vessels in
the proximity of her own coast.

Our Foreign Ministry claimed, finally, that the "control and
protection of navigation on the Atlantic coast" was not being
required simultaneously with other Latin American nations,
and thus appeared to be a special obligation—exclusively Argentine. To subject the delivery of war material to the question of
the convoy under the Lend-Lease Act, constituted a discrimination, since similar conditions had not been imposed on the other
republics having received or having been promised the same aid.

The Department of State adduced in this argument that the
obligation of convoy was not exclusively for the Argentine, since
the other nineteen American republics had declared war on the
Axis or had broken relations, having taken, in accordance with
their means, "drastic measures to eliminate Axis activity within
their frontiers." The United States, in consequence of her intention to aid those American republics that had placed themselves
in the first line of continental defense, was making available to
them all the disposable material, while, on the other hand, denying aid to the governments making no effective contribution to
the American cause. Only by collaborating in some practical and
effective way could the Argentine Republic "legitimately share
in the supplies of armaments available . . . for distribution
among the other American republics."

Regarding the requirement of convoy, the Argentine reaction was immediate. Ruiz Guiñazú cabled Espil, ordering him to make manifest to the North American authorities—even soliciting for it an audience with President Roosevelt—the "incompatibility existing between the suggestions [of convoy] and the oft repeated Argentine position." Espil requested the audience and prepared a memorandum narrating the process of the negotiations. Presentation of the document was made March 24. On April 3 the Department of State acknowledged receipt and insisted that if the Argentine government found acceptable the proposal for control and protection of navigation and would be disposed to carry it out, a basic agreement be negotiated immediately to supply the materials and facilities for the year 1942.

Ruiz Guiñazú rejected the new proposal for control and protection of navigation on the Argentine coast for, after considering the projected text again with the minister of the navy, he did not find any "motive for modifying the position already assumed and communicated which, in consequence, we must maintain." At the same time he ordered Espil to desist in the interview with Roosevelt.

The deterioration of their dealings became even more evident. The Foreign Ministry delivered a note to the North American ambassador in which it criticized the exclusively Argentine obligation of convoy, unacceptable to the government insofar as it "supposes the creation of a state of belligerency which the country does not want and for which it is not prepared." It was expected that the difficulties in the present negotiations would finally be overcome; at the same time the United States government was informed that for the purpose of facilitating every useful contribution in the present situation of the continent, Argentina had just ordered the transfer of the tanker Esso-Formosa to the North American flag.

As a conclusive reply, Hull sent a "strong note" in which he rejected the idea of the "exclusive obligation of convoy" to which he subordinated the benefits of Lend-Lease. He finally affirmed that his government regretted to find it impossible to sign the agreement. Everything ended hopelessly.

The reasons given by the Department of State, Espil reported, for not even signing a plan of military collaboration were the following: the possibility of an alliance between Argentina and the United States against the Axis nations was remote and improbable—a suspicion confirmed by the international attitude of Argentina which, in spite of the recommendation of Rio, acknowledged the purpose of maintaining a policy of strict neutrality. The Department of State thereby considered that the improbable eventuality of a conflict between Argentina and the enemies of the United States did not warrant a movement of arms to that country, for this situation was less important than that surrounding the plans of defense collaboration—particularly in critical moments of pressing military necessities on various fronts and wherever the production of armaments had not yet achieved a rhythm that could satisfy these demands. There was the concern that signing a plan of continental defense collaboration would create in our government, and within our public opinion, the false idea of a moral obligation to provide these arms. But what weighed fundamentally in the decision of the Department of State was the fear of repercussion from any publicity in the other countries of the continent should it happen that, in spite of Argentine isolation, war materials were being provided to our government under the same conditions as those of countries that had broken relations with the Axis or had declared war.

Armour received the cutting note from Hull but did not present it. He had had an interview with the President, with whom he discussed the problem of convoy, and obtained the promise that the question would again be examined with the foreign minister. Armour was then informed by Minister of the Interior Culaciati that Castillo had mentioned the matter to him, from which he deduced that the issue was under serious consideration. In view of this, Armour cabled Hull, suggesting that he "postpone the delivery of the note to the Foreign Ministry while we have time to see if the government intends to do something." In reply, Hull sent this laconic message to his ambassador: "Please present the Department's note."

THE CONSEQUENCES

Argentina thus remained on the margin of the Lend-Lease Act and of the economic and financial assistance the United States was giving to its South American allies. If the task of Castillo and Ruiz Guiñazú to reconcile neutralism with North American aid had some possibility before Pearl Harbor, there is no doubt that the attempt was condemned to frustration after the Japanese attack and the attitude of our delegation at Rio. With the breakdown of negotiations the zig-zagging international policy of Argentina came to rest in a defined position: the maintenance of neutrality to the point of impairing the development of our army and navy. The attitude of the country in the Rio de Janeiro conference had inevitably led to this position of proud isolation, which would definitely separate it from Yankee aid—from the "diplomacy of loans," as Ruiz Guiñazú would disdainfully call it.

All this had produced intense repercussions within the Argentine armed forces. Although a sector of the forces was in agreement with the position of nonbelligerency taken by the government, it is likewise true that the envy of and rivalry with the better-armed neighboring countries, as well as the burdensome responsibility of maintaining the neutrality under such stress, had affected all the officers. This was obvious in the urgings of the military ministries to seek a solution for the increasing military imbalance that was operating against Argentina. In this concern the two great tendencies dividing the army had come together. In August 1942 a memorandum from Generals Tonazzi and Pierrestegui, minister of war and chief of the general staff, pointed out that the strategic balance of the River Plate Basin had been broken and against us. General Ramírez, the representative of the opposing tendency, reached the same conclusion when shortly after taking office as the new minister of war, he again presented to Castillo the Tonazzi-Pierrestegui memorandum. Thus, it is possible to explain the attempts at acquiring arms, especially certain indispensable arms (antitank material, aviation gasoline), from Germany, of which the Blue Book takes account.

In 1942 the Argentine military acquired a sudden and real importance, for the problem of defense had come to the fore. With a continent at war, Argentine neutralism had made military conflict a serious possibility where before it had been entirely hypothetical. On more than one occasion there was serious talk of the possibility of a clash in arms with neighboring countries. There was also the risk of suffering at any moment the consequences of pressures which, on account of the inferiority of the material, the country would not be in condition to resist.

The support from the Lend-Lease system had struck down the balance of forces existing in South America before the war. The case of Brazil is illustrative. In spite of the prevalence of large groups of Germans and Italians, the policy of Brazilian dictator Getulio Vargas was frankly opposed to the Axis. Although of complete Fascist inspiration, one of the principal objectives of his foreign policy consisted in maintaining close relations with the United States. His intervention in the war was definite because it reached the point of sending an expeditionary force to the European front. The benefits Brazil acquired from this collaboration were enormous. In the military field it reequipped the totality of its armed forces. It is sufficient to say that Brazil alone received more than two-thirds of all the wartime aid sent to Latin America, thus forming in the military aspect the first power of South America, at the expense of Argentina.

In addition, an agreement was reached according to which Pan American Airways was permitted to construct air fields in Brazil under the supervision of the United States Engineer Corps and under the condition that these bases would be conceded to Brazil six months after the termination of the war. On the same conditions, major works were undertaken in the ports of Recife and Bahia to be utilized by the North American South Atlantic Fleet. Of no less importance was the economic and technical aid received for the production of Brazil's own war material, such as occurred with the munitions factories and the shipyards for vessels of war. Thus when three destroyers were delivered to the service, and when two others along with a patrol boat were launched in November 1943 during a ceremony carried out in the shipyards of Ilha das Cobras, facing Rio de Janeiro—it could be established that these six vessels were of Brazilian construction.

The aid was not limited to the military aspect only, but was also extended to the economic strengthening of Brazil. In accordance with the resolutions of the Rio de Janeiro conference, the Brazilian Minister of Finance Souza Costa and North American officials signed March 3, 1942, a series of important agreements. They agreed on a program of mobilizing the means of production in Brazil through a credit line of 100 million dollars, which the Export-Import Bank would authorize. Officials of the latter establishment and those of the Metals Reserve Company signed agreements with the Brazilian minister of finance and the British ambassador for the exploitation development of the Itabira Mines and the Victoria Mines Railroad in order to induce large-scale production and transportation of iron. Finally, Souza Costa and Acting Secretary of State Welles signed an agreement establishing a fund of 5 million dollars with the Rubber Reserve Company to be used in collaboration with the government of Brazil for the development of raw rubber production in the

Amazon Valley and adjacent regions. This agreement was accompanied by another, whereby the Rubber Reserve Company would acquire the entire production of Brazilian crude rubber for a period of five years.

The basis of the negotiations undertaken by Foreign Minister Aranha and Hull called for a series of studies to finance the construction of a steel plant in Brazil. Following the recommendation of the Department of State in July 1941, the Export-Import Bank authorized a loan of 45 million dollars for the construction of a Brazilian steel industry. From here came Volta Redonda.

While Brazil victoriously refuted the doctrines that point out the incompatibility between war and progress (A. J. Toynbee, J. U. Neff) Argentina stagnated in an anachronistic ideological attitude, which in fact postponed her advance.

5: THE REVOLUTION OF 1943

RECOGNITION

The foreign policy of the Conservative regime was one of strict neutrality: first, concerning the war in its European phase; second, extension of the conflict to the American hemisphere. After the conference of Rio de Janeiro, only two of the twenty-one American republics maintained relations with the Axis: Argentina and Chile. However, the latter abandoned this position on January 20, 1943. Two days later, in order to reaffirm his solitary neutralism, Castillo declared that the Argentine attitude would remain unalterable and independent of the decisions taken by the other American republics.

Nevertheless, the June 4 revolution reopened this question, which up to that point apparently had been settled. Much has been said of the "rupturist" intentions of the official candidate Robustiano Patrón Costas as a cause of the revolution. However, the truth is that the new government took a series of measures which, at the time, gave rise to the presumption of the initiation of an international policy in accordance with the Pan-American postulates.

In principle, the new government did not manifest any hostility toward the United States. On the contrary, the majority of the military leaders, in spite of the German sympathies of a certain sector, had serious motives of complaint against the Castillo regime—against its weakness, corruption and, above all, its incapacity to obtain arms from the United States and its having allowed Brazil to forge ahead of Argentina in this respect.

102

It is otherwise problematic that in June 1943 Washington would have remained faithful to automatic recognition of *de facto* governments if the nationalist leaders had emphatically announced the continuation of the neutralist policy of Castillo. The attitude of strong pressure from the Department of State in connection with later political events in Argentina clearly proves this.

In the revolutionary proclamation itself there was mention of "making effective an absolute, true, and loyal union in American collaboration and in the fulfillment of international pacts and agreements." Rawson, in his short tenure, assured British Minister Hadow, as well as the secretary of the Paraguayan legation, Edmundo Tombeur (commissioned by the Diplomatic Corps, then meeting in the Chilean Embassy), that Argentina would reintegrate immediately with the American unity, breaking relations with the Axis powers. The ephemeral President promised the same in a telephone conversation with Ambassador Espil in Washington.

The withdrawal of José María Rosa, the principal owner of *El Pampero*, and Horacio Calderón, both on the North American and English black lists, as well as such ministers of the pro-German tendency as Generals Martínez and Pistarini from the Cabinet of Rawson—plus the later inclusion of Admirals Storni and Galíndez, of Colonels Anaya and Jorge Santamarina, all well known as pro-Ally in the Cabinet of Ramírez—demonstrate the evident desire of avoiding frictions for the new government, still without diplomatic recognition. Y. F. Rennie believes that the Rawson Cabinet was a great mistake for a government in search of recognition by the United States.

In his inaugural address of June 7, Ramírez insisted on a policy of friendship and collaboration with the American nations in accordance with existing pacts. With respect to the rest of the world, on the other hand, he characterized it as neutrality, "in the present." On his part, the newly named Foreign Minister Storni was even more explicit:

> Bit by bit, the actions of the Argentine government will continue the policy of American solidarity . . . Argentina will arrive where it must be in international relations. The foreign policy of Argentina will imply a meticulous fulfillment of her obligations with the American countries.

As stipulated in Decree 75 of June 10, language in code or cipher was suspended in international radio-telephonic and radio-telegraph communications, fulfilling thus Resolution XL of Rio de Janeiro. This decision of the Revolutionary government produced an excellent impression in Washington.

The American countries began a series of consultations among themselves on the attitude to be taken with regard to the Argentine situation. The prevailing opinion was that the new government was exercising effective control in all the territory of the Republic and, therefore, that it ought to be recognized. In particular, the Brazilian government expressed its firm conviction that if diplomatic relations continued, it would become easier for the other American republics, identified as they were with the cause of the United Nations, to exercise a favorable influence on Argentine foreign policy. On June 9 Bolivia, Brazil, Chile, and Paraguay officially recognized the government that had risen from the revolution; Germany, Spain, and Italy followed on the next day, June 10; United States, Great Britain, and other American republics on June 11. In the press conference of the same day, Secretary of State Hull qualified the recognition of the military government as a "routine" step, and he emphasized that he "had the benefit of their public declarations of future policy."

Evidently the first acts of the new regime did not disturb Washington. But from then on the June Revolution would have its own law: the fight for power would raise the question of foreign policy and the exalted nationalism would continue to alienate from the government the moderate upholders of diplomatic rupture. With the winners of this fight the country would challenge the United States and would confront her even in the hour of her maximum victory.

THE PROMISED RUPTURE

Cordell Hull, in his memoirs:

In conversations with Ambassador Armour, Ramírez and Storni indicated that, given a comparatively short time in which to prepare the country, the new Government intended to break relations with the Axis. Ramírez thought this would be done by August 15 at the latest. The Argentine Government, they said, intended to implement a policy of close inter-American cooperation based upon the inter-American pacts in force.

Taking up this last phrase, we outlined to Ambassador Armour on June 18 some of the steps we thought the new Argentine Government should take if it meant to offer convincing evidence of its sincerity. These were: to break diplomatic relations with the Axis; to take additional steps to prohibit the use of code for radio communications; to control effectively subversive activities; to stop leaks of funds and strategic materials to the Axis; to control clandestine radio stations within Argentina; to control press and radio propaganda within Argentina along with newsprint to Axis organs; to supervise carefully both civil and commercial aviation; to control foreign funds; to cooperate more effectively with regard to our black list of Axis-connected firms; to cut off financial and commercial relations with the Axis . . . to reduce sharply the amount of pesos then being made available to the Axis Embassies.

All these steps could be justified on the basis of inter-American accords which Argentina had signed but had never really carried out. The fact that we had to list so many indicated the extent to which Argentina was still maintaining relations of all kinds with the Axis.

Within the Revolutionary government the conflict over rupture had already been set loose with violence. Welles refers to the fact that Ramírez repeatedly informed Armour about having finally obtained sufficient support from the most important military chiefs so that his government could break relations with the Axis. On two occasions he even mentioned precise dates. Nevertheless, continues Welles, sudden changes in military personnel kept preventing the carrying out of the promise. In reality Ramírez was trying to locate himself between the two extreme goups that were fighting among themselves, but just as the nationalists within the military were increasing their power, he was gradually losing control of the situation. The initial commitment to break with the Axis was becoming more and more difficult to carry out. From Buenos Aires Ambassador Armour reported to his superiors that within the government many elements opposed to the rupture were beginning to appear.

Storni, on his part, continued with his task of convincing Washington that Argentina would cooperate in the hemispheric program. On the occasion of the anniversary of North American independence he said: "Every nation that tries to disturb our solidarity and continental union is not with Argentina but is against Argentina." Four days later he sent a letter to Uruguayan Vice President Guani, president of the Committee of Political Defense, located in Montevideo, promising that the Ramírez government would review its foreign policy in the light of the Rio de Janeiro agreements.

But skepticism seemed to prevail in the Department of State. According to their opinion, the fact that Argentina still lagged by the end of July in breaking relations with the Axis was enough of an indication that the new regime would not modify the foreign policy of its predecessor. Hull cabled Armour July 27 to return to Washington for a conference in which "the whole question of our relations with Argentina" would be reviewed.

STORNI'S LETTER

When Armour interviewed Chancellor Storni on July 29, he informed him that he had been called to Washington for a consultation. He asked him for a clear declaration on the Argentine position, preferably in writing. He also recalled to him his own promises as well as those of Ramírez on rupture with the Axis by August 15. When Ramírez was consulted, and then agreed to the sending of a confidential letter to Cordell Hull explaining to him the Argentine situation, Storni, with the help of Foreign Ministry officials, among them Undersecretary Gache, drafted a protocol letter announcing the change of attitude manifested in the government after the revolution, as well as the efforts made to line up with the Allies. He then carried a draft to the presidency, where it was held for a certain time. There was talk of sending a special envoy with the letter but, after several days, the definitive text was returned to the Foreign Ministry. This text, retaining only the initial and final paragraphs, contained an introduction of changes that did not belong to the Storni draft.

In the letter it was explained at great length why Argentina could not break relations with the Axis. The sentiment of our country, it said, eminently American and firmly opposed to totalitarian regimes, was on the side of the United Nations in spirit and in practice. But one could not coldly drag the Argentine conscience to a rupture of diplomatic relations without a previous preparation. With the Axis inexorably defeated, the letter continued, this unexpected rupture would submit Argentine chivalry to a harsh test. This brings to mind the judgment merited by Italy when, in a similar situation, that country took the same kind of initiative with regard to a defeated France.

Storni denied that the Argentine Revolutionary regime sympathized with the Axis. He insisted that his government would spare no efforts to comply with obligations assumed. But he could not do so without a cause that would justify it. To act otherwise would be to provide arguments for those who might think that he was operating under pressure or threat from foreign agents. And this would be tolerated neither by the people nor by the armed forces of the country. He concluded with a veiled reference to the North American intention of changing the "balance" of power in South America:

> I can affirm to you . . . that the Axis countries have nothing to hope for from our Government and that public opinion is daily more unfavorable to them. But this evolution would be more rapid and effective for the American cause if President Roosevelt should make a gesture of genuine friendship toward our people; such a gesture might be the urgent provision of airplanes, spare parts and machinery to restore Argentina to the position of equilibrium to which it is entitled with respect to other South American countries.

The request for military material made it evident that the shortage of arms was still an unsolved problem; on the contrary, it had become aggravated with the passage of time. Shortly after the removal of General Rawson, his successors had considered sending him as head of a mission to Washington, and in this regard Espil sounded out the North American authorities. But the Department of State replied that as long as the Argentine government did not break with the Axis, any conversation about armaments would be useless.

Storni's letter closed with a plea for understanding and friendship on the part of the United States toward the Ramírez government during its difficult initial period.

Armour himself delivered the letter to Hull on August 14.

Four days later Espil reported that during discussions with Armour in Washington the latter had advanced the idea that "everything makes him [Armour] believe the answer will clash with some of our arguments, and that it will stress the necessity of maintaining without essential modification the policy that this government has been following with Argentina."

Hull answered Storni's note in a most scathing manner. The reply was, according to Smith, one of the most severe diplomatic censures ever aimed at a Latin American government by the Department of State. The magazine *Time* (September 20, 1943) compared it to a "polished" and "cutting" razor.

The secretary of state expressed his satisfaction that the Argentine people felt themselves indissolubly linked with the other inhabitants of the American hemisphere. Nevertheless, continued the note, it is with regret that the North American government and the people of the United States have had to conclude that the indubitable sentiments of the Argentine people have not been translated into the fulfillment of obligations freely contracted by their government together with the other American countries. He mentioned a number of resolutions which Argentina had not fulfilled, emphasizing that the Buenos Aires government was the only one in America to maintain relations with the Axis. The Ramírez government's failure to abide by its commitments was the reason why Argentina's international position was being interpreted erroneously.

Hull conceded that only the Argentine government could determine the extent to which public opinion would support a change in foreign policy. But he expressed his surprise that fulfillment with contracted obligations could be a motive for considering such action to have been taken under the pressure of foreign agencies, when the obligations had all been freely subscribed to by the American republics and had been fulfilled by all except Argentina.

He thought it necessary to point out that the private and public declarations made by President Ramírez and by Storni during the first weeks of the government gave the North Americans sufficient reason to anticipate that the Argentine sentiments of continental solidarity, as well as her adherence to inter-American obligations, would in a short time become translated into an effective action.

He admitted that the products of Argentine agriculture and mining were of the greatest utility for the cause of the United Nations, but he observed that very highly remunerative prices had been paid for them. He also claimed the United Nations had refrained from taking advantage of the fact that, because of their military and naval efficiency, they were the only possible markets for Argentina. Regarding the suggestion that the United States could supply airplanes, spare parts, and machinery, he answered:

> The supply of arms and munitions . . . is exclusively for the purpose of contributing to the defense of the Hemisphere. . . . Since Argentina, both by its words and its actions, has indicated clearly that the Argentine armed forces will not under present conditions be used in a manner designed to forward the cause of the security of the New World, and thereby the vital interests of the United States, it would be impossible for the President of the United States to enter into an agreement to furnish arms and munitions to Argentina under the Lend-Lease Act.

As to the disturbance of South American equilibrium, he replied that the raising of the military and naval balance issues certainly appeared inconsistent with the inter-American doctrine of peaceful solution of international disputes, to which doctrine the Argentine publicists had made so many practical contributions.

The publication of Hull's letter in the Argentine newspapers inflamed nationalist sentiments. Leaflets against Storni were scattered in the heart of the city—leaflets written and printed by the conspiratorial military group GOU. *Noticias Gráficas,* which had dared to publish an editorial condemning the neutralist attitude of the government, was ordered closed and the edition confiscated. The position of Storni was made unbearable, and he had to resign on the following day. The *New York Herald Tribune* headlined Storni's resignation, and so did the *New York Times,* noting the American rejection of the arms request. As the situation of the chief of state himself was compromised, Storni sent him a letter assuming full responsibility for the document. On the same day the presidency of the nation, through a communiqué, declared that the "historical tradition of a nation . . . cannot be weakened by the confidential expressions of a functionary."

In reality Hull's answer was a model of crudeness. Storni was the principal pro-Ally figure favoring rupture within the Cabinet, which was perfectly well known in the Department of State. On the other hand, Ramírez as well found himself between the two bands that were disputing power. The fact that Hull grasped at the opportunity offered to him by Storni's ingenuous note to discredit the Revolutionary government had thrown Ramírez into the arms of the extreme nationalists. Hull's satisfaction turned out to be very costly. The only consequence was to increase the anti-American sentiment within the government and among its supporters, as well as to increase the authority and prestige of the strongest nationalist elements. The expostulation from Washington jolted the military government and intensified the differences already existing among some of its ministers—with all the advantage falling to the partisans of the neutralist position, demonstrating that a policy of rapprochement with Washington was proving itself impossible without previously passing through the trailing gallows of humiliation.

THE RUPTURE

After Hull's unfortunate reply to Storni's letter, the ultranationalist faction made ready for the final assault on power. Within the government there still remained some moderates who upheld the necessity for lining up with the United Nations. On October 12 Farrell was designated vice president of the nation. Two days later the minister of finance, Jorge Santamarina, resigned; then Admiral Galíndez, minister of public works; and then General Anaya, minister of education. General Gilbert became the new foreign minister.

The war had favored regional agreements such as those agreed upon in the conference of the River Plate States in 1941. Under the Conservative regime, the policy of economic rapprochement received special attention, a tendency that was accentuated even more under the Ramírez government. Even earlier, during the administration of Admiral Storni, on occasion of the visit of the Chilean Chancellor Fernández y Fernández to Buenos Aires, a plan had been agreed upon for the study and proposal of bases for a customs union along with a convention on trade and travel (July 24, 1943).

The group of military officers whose preponderance in the army had been strengthened by the events of October had redoubled their efforts to establish economic and political relations with the small nations bordering on Argentina. Without doubt, the rivalry with Brazil in this matter was one of the dominant motives. But they were also convinced that Argentina ought to be the monitor nation of South America. Also, the purpose was certainly not far from their design to break down the isolation in which the intransigent neutralism had placed the country. At the same time, behind all this lay the creation of a counterprogram, which might combat North American influence in South America. That constant of Argentine foreign policy, which is anti-Yankeeism, was presented now in a novel and aggressive version.

The military group, however, was not thinking only of rapprochement with other countries by means of agreements undertaken through official channels—such as the commercial treaty and customs union negotiated with Paraguay on occasion of the visit to Buenos Aires of President Morínigo and his Foreign Minister Argaña, whereby that country which had been leaning toward Brazil returned again to the sphere of Argentine influence. There would also be recourse to subversive action and attempts to establish governments sympathizing with Argentina in the neighboring countries. These steps were not undertaken, as was logical, through the Foreign Ministry, but by means of the military attachés accredited to the respective countries. Hull refers to the fact that in the middle of August "we were receiving reports that the Argentine government was sending military emissaries to Uruguay, Bolivia, and Chile in an endeavor to win over the armies of those countries to the Argentine point of view."

On December 20 in Bolivia a revolutionary movement dislodged General Peñaranda and replaced him by Major Gualberto Villarroel. In the preparation of this episode, there was collaboration from the leaders of the *Movimiento Nacionalista Revolucionario*—among them Víctor Paz Estenssoro, linked to the Argentine military—and also from the *Partido Izquierdista Revolucionario*. Although the new government hastened to issue a declaration in which it reaffirmed its intention of complying with its international obligations, as well as of maintaining the decisions taken by the former government—such as the declaration of war on the Axis—the United States did not proceed to an automatic recognition, as in the Argentine case. Hull conceded that a North American recognition policy with respect to the hemisphere was in gestation.

Argentina, on its part, did not delay in recognizing the Bolivian government. In support of Hull's reservations, on December 22, the Uruguayan Vice President Alberto Guani, president of the Committee for Political Defense, created by the Rio conference and headquartered in Montevideo, announced that any government established by force during the war ought not to be recognized until the other American countries had carried out consultations to decide if it appeared disposed to comply with inter-American obligations and, furthermore, if it was of native inspiration. This doctrine, later known as the "Guani Doctrine," was communicated immediately to all the members of the Pan-American system, with the obvious exception of Argentina and Bolivia, along with enemies of the defense of the American the Department of State had evidence that elements foreign to Bolivia, along with enemies of the defense of the American republics, had inspired the recent revolution. Since he had sent a memorandum to President Roosevelt on January 12, 1944, in which he informed him of the alarm of Argentina's neighbors on account of the activities of the subversive agents of Ramírez, Roosevelt ordered a considerable increase in the shipment of arms and munitions for the Brazilian government. Days later the South Atlantic Fleet made a visit to the Uruguayan capital.

The investigation, which was carried out in accordance with the prescriptions of the Montevideo Committee for Defense, demonstrated that the new band of army majors in Bolivia—already masters of power—among whose members figured various persons linked to the Axis, had been aided and supported by Argentine military. Without ignoring the evident discontent with the Peñaranda administration and the characteristic political instability of Bolivia as causes of the revolution, there remained no doubt whatsoever that the Bolivian military had received aid from their Argentine colleagues.

By January 21 the Department of State had prepared a confidential memorandum outlining the active participation of the Argentine government in the Bolivian upheaval. At the same time, the decision not to recognize the new government was based on this document. If Roosevelt approved it, it would be delivered to the press for publication, after which strong economic sanctions would be imposed on Argentina, among them probably the freezing of balances due our country on deposit in the United States.

The news produced consternation in the government. Apart from the logical inconvenience of the blocking, the denunciation of the complicity in the Bolivian revolution would prejudice the prestige of the country in the rest of America. Its position, already precarious, would be weakened even further with the North American accusation of intervention in the internal affairs of another country.

Independently of all this, another event occurring in the first days of November 1943 had complicated Argentina's international panorama. This was in Trinidad when the Argentine consul, Oscar Alberto Hellmuth, was detained by the English while on service travel to Europe. In reply to the pertinent protest from the Foreign Ministry, the British Foreign Office reported that the detention was due to the fact that the position of the consul as enemy agent had been established. In reality, Hellmuth, although an Argentine citizen, was an agent of the RSHA (Reichs-Sicherheitshauptamt), a secret espionage and police organization directed by Himmler. He had entered into contact with the higher Argentine military and had been commissioned to negotiate in Germany the procurement of arms and other indispensable war materials, as well as the safe conduct of the tanker *Buenos Aires* then tied up in Götenburg. So that he might carry out his mission, he had been designated assistant consul in Barcelona in October 1943. This matter, although limited to a transaction between the Foreign Ministries, incurred the serious risk of converting itself into a scandal.

The Ramírez government learned that the Department of State would deliver to the press on February 24, for immediate publication, the copy of the memorandum in which the Argentine intrigues in the successful *coup* of Villarroel were detailed. Besides publication of the memorandum, the news had already reached Buenos Aires regarding the freezing of funds. In fact, the Treasury Department had already given such confidential advice on the imminence of the measure to the North American banks operating in Argentina, and the latter in transmitting it to their agents in Buenos Aires had alerted the government. All this hastened the course of events and Ramírez, after consulting various advisers, decided to avert at all costs the accusing publication of the Department of State.

Foreign Minister Gilbert tried to gain time when he informed Armour that his government could definitely break relations with the Axis, but that in reciprocity Washington ought to give up every measure that could be interpreted as coercion on his government. The request was destined to deprive of arguments the ultranationalist band within the army, making it appear that the rupture was a free and independent act. Armour's report on the Argentine decision to break relations had held up the broadside that Washington prepared. Roosevelt ordered the suppression of the allusions contained in the memorandum, and when it was given to the press that afternoon it appeared only as a severe reprimand to the Bolivian regime, to which diplomatic recognition was denied, and did not include a single word of censure against the Argentine government.

Ramírez, supported by a group of officers who were then occupying the place left by the moderates, decided to take the definitive step. There is no doubt that Washington's attitude hastened his decision, but the fact ought not be underrated that in his mind, as well as in the minds of those who supported him, the course of the war had been weighed: Hitler had suffered serious reverses in his campaign against Russia and had been obliged to abandon Africa; the Allies, after invading Italy, had obtained her surrender, and hence the consequent downfall of Fascism.

On January 26, 1944, the government broke diplomatic relations with Germany and Japan. As a pretext the government gave the discovery of an extensive espionage network in Argentine territory and also took advantage of Hellmuth's participation in it. Besides the arrests, there followed a series of restrictive measures against the Axis, such as the suspension of commercial-financial relations and the communications by telegraph, telephone, and radio.

Nevertheless, Ramírez encountered strong resistance within his own government. Several ministers resigned. The nominal rupture could not be carried out as an effective rupture. On February 15 Gilbert found himself obliged to give up the post of foreign minister, and ten days later, after a tumultuous meeting in the Deliberative Council—attended by the President and delegates of the garrisons at Campo de Mayo, Buenos Aires, and El Palomar—Ramírez, deprived of all military support, delegated his office to Vice President Farrell.

HULL'S WRATH

In order to maintain the continuity of the regime, and thereby prevent the United States and other governments from having to decide about recognition, precautions were taken to surround the departure of Ramírez with all the appearances of a voluntary delivery of his position in favor of the Vice President. Ramírez signed a document whereby he simply delegated his presidential functions.

Farrell's new government did not delay in informing the American community that it would continue supporting the cause of the United Nations, especially since the regime had broken relations with Germany and Japan. Thus it was believed that there would be no change in the diplomatic relations between Argentina and the rest of the American countries. Nevertheless, Cordell Hull thought the contrary.

That the Argentine Revolutionary government was an ally of the Axis constituted an article of faith for Hull. He was convinced that only a policy of pressure could save the program of hemispheric solidarity. His view of the Argentine situation in

1944 was the following: he identified the strong anti-Yankee sentiment and the clearly resolute Argentine foreign policy as a sinister collaboration with the Germans and Japanese. In fairness to these prejudices, there was undeniably a sympathy for the Axis within broad military and civilian sectors. But Hull attributed greater importance to Fascism and Nazism than to a nationalism based, above all, on a marked antipathy for the United States. And upon these premises the Department of State arranged its conduct with respect to Argentina. Furthermore, Hull harbored a personal resentment toward our country. Welles says:

> Argentina had long been a "pain in the neck" to the three or four members of the Department of State who were then determining the hemispheric policy of the United States. The constitutional governments of President Justo, of President Castillo, and even of President Ortiz had, at a succession of inter-American conferences, frequently opposed United States delegations on questions of policy. This had brought about injured susceptibilities and a very personal resentment on the part of the guiding influences in the Department of State. The feeling of hostility toward Argentina was notorious and had been made increasingly apparent.

Regarding the latest Argentine events, the United States considered the new government as one arising from a *coup d'etat*. Washington maintained the thesis that had been applied to the Bolivian case: no government could enter into official relations with Buenos Aires until the pertinent consultations had been carried out among the other American countries through the Committee of Political Defense in Montevideo. Argentina brandished the Estrada Doctrine as the only valid one in matters of recognition and charged that Hull's steps were a direct intervention in its internal affairs. On March 4 Stettinius, as acting secretary of state, gave to the press a declaration reporting that since Ramírez had been deposed by groups opposed to hemispheric cooperation, the North American ambassador in Buenos Aires had received instructions to suspend relations with the new regime. Accordingly the Department was awaiting developments. The following day, Eden, in the House of Commons, confirmed that in view of the obscurity surrounding the delegation of power by Ramírez to the Vice President, the British ambassador had been instructed in the sense of limiting his relations with the new government to questions of mere transactions.

Nevertheless, the hopes of the Department of State to obtain from the American republics a unanimous support for its policy of consultation with respect to the recognition of the Farrell government disappeared when, at the beginning of March, Chile, Paraguay, and Bolivia established diplomatic relations with Argentina. Until the end of June, there was no change in the situation; the other countries did not establish official relations, but neither did they withdraw their diplomatic missions from Buenos Aires nor impose economic sanctions on Argentina.

On June 10, four days after the disembarkation of the Allies in Normandy—and when the war took a definitive turn—Colonel Juan Domingo Perón delivered a speech on the occasion of inaugurating the Chair of National Defense in the University of La Plata. He affirmed that, for Argentina, there would exist no difference between an Allied victory or an Axis victory, and that in one or the other case Argentina could reach its legitimate national aspirations only by means of a vigorous diplomacy, supported by the military power, and by a government that would exercise dominion over each and every phase of national life. Because the speech was given after the Normandy invasion and came from the man with greatest power in Argentina, Perón's challenging words signified a true threat to Washington. It was without doubt a serious warning that the Argentine government would not change its attitude.

Hull understood that the United States would have to take a

decision regarding the Argentine case. Since the prevailing formula of nonrecognition could easily have been a symptom of weakness, Ambassador Armour was called to Washington June 22, and on the following day Hull sent a memorandum to the other American governments, affirming that the Farrell regime had lent open and notorious aid to the enemies of the United Nations. They were informed that the ambassador of the United States had been withdrawn, and they were asked to make a similar decision.

But for the program of coercion adopted by the Department of State, the collaboration of Great Britain was needed—it was indispensable that the British ambassador be withdrawn. The English, however, were not in agreement to interrupt diplomatic relations with Argentina. Concerned about their extensive capital investment in the country, they did not want to see themselves deprived of representation; it was of particular interest to them to renew the convention [that would expire at the end of August] in order to acquire the exportable balance of Argentine meat. On June 3, 1944, the British foreign minister had instructed the ambassador in Washington, Lord Halifax, to negotiate with Hull the abandonment of a "diplomatic victory" over the Argentine government and to underscore the necessity of planting its recognition in clear and fixed terms. According to these instructions, he was to oppose "energetically" every North American request to withdraw the British ambassador from Buenos Aires.

In spite of this Hull pressed the measure on the British government. Although Churchill preferred to do it so as to avoid adding to the already numerous differences with the Department of State, Eden showed himself obstinate to this initiative; and only the personal intervention of President Roosevelt on June 30 made possible that Great Britain would go along with the United States in its political sanction against the Revolutionary government.

Toward the month of July, Argentina carried out various attempts to obtain recognition from the United States and with it to bring to an end the diplomatic pressure she was suffering. The Argentine chancellor sent two memoranda to the Department of State, June 22 and July 10, through the Chilean chargé d'affaires at Washington. These documents sought to prove that Argentina had fully complied with her international obligations, and that she had effectively lined up with the other American republics in breaking relations. In reply the Department of State released a declaration on July 26 entitled "Nonrecognition of Argentina." It detailed the reasons for the negativity of the United States in establishing diplomatic relations with the Farrell government and, for Smith, it was as intemperate a reply as that of Hull to Admiral Storni. The declaration proclaimed that the policy followed by Argentina during the war had broken hemispheric unity and signified a positive aid to the enemies of the United Nations. It was clarified that the negative aspect in establishing diplomatic relations did not constitute a direct intervention in Argentine affairs, since this measure was taken by various countries and was based on multilateral agreements signed on behalf of effective hemispheric defense. The determination of the Ramírez regime to break relations with the Axis was nullified, the document continued, by powerful forces within the same government who were opposed to every measure that could complement this action. The Argentine memorandum of July 10 made known that when the Ramírez government took important measures, like that of the rupture of relations, it was immediately deposed for causes not yet known and that, as soon as the new government had taken charge of power, the measures complementary to rupture were interrupted. For the Department of State the two memoranda reinforced the conviction that pro-Nazi elements within the present Argentine government responsible for the downfall of Ramírez had prevented every undertaking against the activities of the Axis. The

North American declaration also analyzed the arguments by which the Farrell regime believed itself worthy of diplomatic recognition. Argentina was invoking full solidarity with the American nations on the basis of a "few acts of the ousted Ramírez government and on mere promises about its future activity."

On July 21 Hull rejected an offer from the Paraguayan government to mediate the Argentine-North American differences. The secretary of state reiterated his well-known thesis that the desertion of the Allied cause on the part of the Argentine government did not constitute a bilateral dispute between Washington and Buenos Aires but that it represented, on the contrary, a rupture between Argentine and the entire American community.

The harsh attitude of the United States put an end to the attempts at rapprochement, which through various channels the Argentine government had been seeking. After learning of the July 26 declaration on the "nonrecognition of Argentina," our government immediately withdrew Ambassador Escobar, who was still residing in Washington. With this, the rupture of relations between the two governments was complete. From now on, resumes Whitaker, the North American historian, both countries would engage in all possible manifestations of bad will short of a declaration of war.

Toward the end of July the Department of State had ready a program of maximum coercion against Argentina. Its objective was to force our government to change the international attitude maintained until then. However, within the Revolutionary regime in Buenos Aires, no one showed any indication of belief that such a thing could happen. The withdrawal of the United States ambassador, as well as those of the other American and European countries, Great Britain included, had marked the first steps. In accordance with this, Argentina was excluded from all the international conferences on the problems of the war and postwar, such as the monetary conference of Bretton Woods and that of civil aviation which took place in Chicago.

In the economic field the already existing restrictions on exportations to Argentina were increased. In September 1944, North American ships were prohibited to visit the Argentine ports. For some time now—and for political reasons—Argentine-North American commerce had descended very much below the normal limits. The United States was the only country with which there was diminution of imports. But the gravity of the pressure was accented still more by the fact that the United States constituted the only market capable of supplying us with indispensable products and materials. On August 16 the Argentine gold deposits, which still remained in the United States, were frozen inasmuch as the Revolutionary government had already begun in October 1943 to repatriate them from the Federal Reserve Bank of New York to the Central Bank of Buenos Aires.

But no economic sanction could be taken against Argentina without English collaboration, and this Cordell Hull knew perfectly well. There is no doubt that the independent international position of Argentina during the Second World War was based in a singular manner on the close financial and commercial links between our country and England. The explanation of our foreign policy in this period cannot disregard the complex triangle of Anglo-Argentine-North American relations. There are diverse reasons why Great Britain sought to maintain at all cost good relations with Argentina. If London's attitude were too rigid, the important British investments would become convenient hostages for the Buenos Aires government. Besides, the British population and army were then depending on our meat. But, above all, the principal objective of British policy was to conserve a preponderant position in Argentina for the postwar world, ever coming closer. England wanted to avoid the possibility that the process of liquidating its political influence, accelerated by the war, would also reach the River Plate.

The other leg of the triangle, the Anglo-American relations, were in turn bristling with difficulties: problems between the two countries were enormous. Churchill wrote to Eden February 27, 1944, when Hull requested him not to recognize the Farrell government. Noting all the difficulties with the United States, Churchill stressed the necessity of demonstrating friendship through support of United States policy in Latin America.

But English aid was not always present, and the Argentine case was a confirmation of this fact. In spite of the pressures from Hull, the British resisted taking any step beyond nonrecognition and the withdrawal of the ambassador. On July 14 the British prime minister sent a note to President Roosevelt in which he informed him that although his government wanted to cooperate in his policy with the South American countries, the United Kingdom depended on the Argentine market because it imported 40 per cent of its quota of meat and could not run the risk of losing this source of supply.

The difficulties between the Foreign Office and the Department of State grew even sharper in the final months of 1944. The motive was the renewal of the meat contract between the United Kingdom and Argentina. During the administration of Ramírez, on July 22, 1943, the British food minister had concluded with the Argentine representative, Cárcano, the purchase of the exportable surplus of meat by means of an agreement that would terminate September 30, 1944. Seven days before this date, Churchill telegraphed Roosevelt informing him that his government would begin negotiations for the renewal of the contract. On August 26 the North American President replied to him hoping that a satisfactory contract would be achieved. In view of this, the food minister requested the Argentine negotiators in London to inquire if their government would be interested in a contract of long duration, that is, four years.

Nevertheless, unexpectedly, in the Second Quebec Conference the North Americans requested the English not to conclude with the Argentines any kind of agreement, not even for two years. Hull deplored the despicable economic advantages of negotiating in the long run with a Fascist government. But the English reasons to conclude the negotiations were very strong. They maintained that if they definitely lost the Argentine supply, their scarce meat rationing would be reduced to two-thirds of the present rations. But what worried them more was that, if they refused the contract, the Argentine government would not find itself in the compromised situation that Hull expected, because other buyers would rapidly appear on the scene to solve the problem. Belgium, Holland, and France, who had gold in abundance, were anxious to acquire great quantities of meat, and this could mean that the international price would go up. For its part Great Britain could not indefinitely restrain these countries, since with anticipation she had informed them of her intention to buy the totality of the existing Argentine beef through a long-term contract so as to then place the surplus in the liberated countries of Europe.

In the face of the North American demand, Churchill maintained that a maximum effort ought to be undertaken and an agreement reached in regard to what was being sought. He suggested to the War Cabinet on October 4 that the problem ought to be expounded again with Hull by expressing to him that the signing of the contract could be postponed until after the North American elections. But Roosevelt cabled, indicating to him his criterion that the United Kingdom, rather than prolonging her contract with Argentina, should proceed only toward renewing month by month the already expired contract.

On October 13 Churchill sent out instructions accordingly. Before learning of them, however, the minister of food was negotiating with the Argentine representatives on the basis of the reply from Buenos Aires favoring the proposal to conclude a convention for four years. Confronted with this change, the minister had to initiate new discussions. In view of the serious risk involved—that if he refused the request of Roosevelt, irritating factors could be introduced into the painful economic and financial negotiations pending with the United States—the United Kingdom abandoned her original project and agreed to the monthly renewal for a period of not more than six months.

To the reticent attitude of the English, there was added the criticism that former Undersecretary of State Sumner Welles was leveling in newspapers and magazines. The muffled rivalry between Hull and Welles had broken out irreconcilably in the Conference of Rio de Janeiro. In effect, both represented in the Argentine case the respectively harsh and bland versions of North American policy. Welles maintained the following:

> The stupidity of the policy adopted lay in the fact that financial or economic coercion by the United States could never be effective in weakening the national economy of Argentina or in creating a financial or economic crisis unless the other American Republics were disposed to cooperate in the imposition of such economic sanctions, and unless Great Britain was willing to take similar action.

Besides, according to the same critic, under the direction of Hull the Good Neighbor Policy had been transformed into something unilateral and domineering, and the old fear of Yankee interventionism had been reborn in America. All the more had Hull turned against the Argentines, demonstrating his impatience with everyone who, within or outside his country, was not disposed to subscribe to his policy of coercion.

The secretary of state on September 7 renewed the charge and affirmed that Argentina was the general headquarters of the Fascist movement in the hemisphere. Two days later President Roosevelt himself became involved in the pressure campaign unleashed by Hull. In the declaration he formulated on this occasion, there was nothing new except the resounding presidential approval of Hull's conduct. It was an official notification that Hull's policy was the policy of his government. In reality the many criticisms and attacks from which Hull was then suffering had created a doubt in public opinion as to whether or not, in the Argentine case, this was actually the expression of his government.

COUNTEROFFENSIVE AND ARRANGEMENT

On October 27, 1944, after consulting the other countries of Latin America, the Argentine government addressed the Pan-American Union and formally requested a consultation meeting of the foreign ministers of all the American counties in order to explain its position and to detail the specific measures taken in the fulfillment of its inter-American obligations.

Welles mentions that the "well-timed Argentine proposal was received with consternation by the Department of State." Even prior to that time the various American countries not in agreement with the situation—and provoked by the Argentine-North American conflict—had begun to consult among themselves. Specifically the government of Mexico, some months before, had requested a meeting of consultation, and according to expectation the suggestion was abruptly rejected by the Department of State.

In reality the Argentine initiative conformed to the letter and the spirit of the inter-American agreements since, as Welles notes, no government could deny that the controversy between the United States and Argentina was placing the system in danger and was threatening the security of the hemisphere.

Hull, at this time ill, was decidedly opposed. He feared that Argentina and perhaps the "few satellite countries of Argentina" would introduce every type of discussion, and that the meeting would be utilized as a means of diplomatic recognition.

Although the Department of State refused our commentary, it soon appeared that the "official position would be that of not acknowledging the request since it did not come from a recognized government." Nevertheless, on October 31 Acting

Secretary of State Stettinius prepared the way by which the Department of State would appear in a broader and more conciliatory attitude. In a press interview he declared that the United States would not be opposed to a meeting of foreign ministers. Two days later it was officially announced that a meeting would take place at an early date, but it seemed likely that the Argentine problem would not be treated since the principal object of the meeting would be to combine the inter-American system with the world organization recently sketched out at Dumbarton Oaks. A strong internal pressure was being felt in the Department of State to find a formula of settlement with the Buenos Aires regime. The same was occuring in some of the other American countries such as Brazil, Chile, and Peru—countries that had already manifested their intention of not attending a meeting in which they might find themselves obliged without alternative to line up against the United States or against Argentina.

Stettinius obtained another argument to disembarrass himself with the burning Argentine request. The Mexican government had requested a meeting of the countries which collaborated in the war. The United States made plain her total agreement with the proposal, showing herself disposed to participate in a conference wherein postwar problems might be discussed, but she also made clear that Argentina, on account of her nonbelligerent condition, could not participate. For this there was recourse to the artifice of inviting to the conference not through the Pan American Union—with which our participation would have been indispensable—but by means of direct agreement reached between the American governments with the exception, of course, of Argentina. The scarcely strict Pan-American system in effect at the moment was supplanted by a direct diplomatic exchange outside the Pan American Union.

The governing board of the organization proposed the consideration of the Argentine request and implied that in the projected conference an opportunity would be offered to consider it. In reply the Farrell government sent a forcible note under date of January 10, informing the board that in the face of disregarding Argentina's rights and of altering the procedures for consultation, Argentina would abstain from attending the meetings which the Pan American Union might organize. But in spite of these bitter manifestations, an agreement had already been reached.

Welles relates the following in *Where Are We Heading?*:

> . . . in February, 1945, the new regime in the Department sent a special mission to Buenos Aires. In the ostensibly secret conversations which there took place with Colonel Perón, Dr. Juan Cooke, and other actual leaders in the Argentine government, it was agreed that if Argentina implemented her hemispheric defense commitments contracted in 1942 at Rio de Janeiro and accepted the opportunity to reenter the fold of the American nations which would be held out to her after the Mexico City conference, the United States would abandon its coercive attitude and cancel all the restrictive measures which had been imposed on economic relations between the two countries. It was clearly understood that military materiel would no longer be withheld. While the suggestion was made that it would be eminently desirable for the military dictatorship to turn the government over to the Argentine Supreme Court until national elections could be held, the suggestion was not pressed, and Colonel Perón steadily refused to make any commitments about what he claimed were purely internal questions.

The Inter-American Conference on Problems of War and Peace took place in the city of Mexico, that is, in the Palace of Chapultepec, February 21 to March 8, 1945. Regarding Argentina—a subject excluded from the official agenda—the delegates agreed that if Argentina would subscribe to the Act of Chapultepec, declare war on the Axis, and give evidence of the fact that she was restraining the activities of the Axis, all the

American republics would officially renew relations with her. The United States, in an individual form, went even further in assuring that, if these measures were taken, the United States was disposed to use her influence in order to obtain the entrance of Argentina into the inauguration of the United Nations.

Resolution LIX, which summed up the prior requirements, signified a green light for the Farrell regime. On March 27, 1945, it declared war on Germany and Japan. Decree 6,945 thus established:

Article 1: The Government of the nation accepts the invitation that has been extended to it by the twenty American Republics participating in the Inter-American Conference on Problems of War and Peace and adheres to the final act of the same.

Article 2: For the purpose of identifying the policy of the nation with that common to the other American Republics and of consolidating with them in the face of threats or acts of aggression from any country toward an American State— be it declared the state of war between the Argentine Republic, on the one hand, and the Empire of Japan on the other.

Article 3: In the same way, be it declared the state of war between the Argentine Republic and Germany, with due regard to the character of the latter as an ally of Japan.

Article 4: Through the respective Ministries and State Secretariats, there will be adopted the measures necessary for the state of belligerency, as well as those needed to put an end definitively to all activity of persons, firms, and enterprises of any nationality that may threaten the security of the State and interfere in the war effort of the United Nations or threaten the peace, the welfare, and the security of the American Nations.

On April 4 the Argentine representative in Mexico signed the Acta Final, and on April 9 the United States, Great Britain, and the other American republics established diplomatic relations with Argentina.

After nearly two years of North American pressure, the military government declared war on the moribund Axis and obligated itself to take energetic measures against their citizens and interests. There is no doubt that Argentina gained by far more than she gave up. She was permitted to sign the Chapultapec agreements and to normalize her relations with all the American states, and she was assured a place as a member of the forthcoming conference of the United Nations. But most important was the fact that the government only months before denounced by Roosevelt himself as a fortress of Fascism in America had remained unchanged in power as master of the situation.

THE SAN FRANCISCO CONFERENCE

Stettinius had promised at Chapultapec that his government would secure the admission of Argentina in the United Nations, so that she might occupy a place in the future world organization. But since all the other American republics had collaborated with the Allies, they were by now invited to the San Francisco meeting.

The character of the charter members of the world organization had already been an object of arduous discussion at Dumbarton Oaks. The United States wanted to include the United Nations and those which without having declared war had aided the war effort. The Russians on their part were opposed to the admission of any country that had not declared war or had not signed the United Nations declaration. As no solution had been found at Dumbarton Oaks, the problem of the charter members was again brought up at Yalta. Stalin wanted a maximum reduction in voting power for the small nations. He felt they would act simply as satellites of the United States in the case of the Latin American republics, or of Great Britain in the case of the countries of the Commonwealth. To offset Stalin's suspicions, Roosevelt agreed that the Soviet republics of White Russia and Ukraine would be admitted as members of the United Nations.

Roosevelt on his part obtained the agreement from Stalin that all the associated nations having declared war before May 1, 1945, would be invited to the San Francisco conference. Stalin's concession did not include Argentina. The North American President himself took on the task of clarifying that our country was not entering in the category of a nation with the right to be invited to San Francisco, for neither had she been a member of the United Nations nor had she collaborated with the Allies. Stettinius recounts in *Roosevelt and the Russians* that at Yalta Stalin, upon the start of negotiations, stated that Argentina ought to be punished for not having cooperated with the Allies, and that if Argentina were in the Soviet sector of the world he would make himself responsible for doing so.

At the time of the San Francisco meeting, the Russian representative immediately solicited that the two Soviet republics of White Russia and the Ukraine be admitted as members of the conference. In his speech he harshly attacked Argentina and again reproached her for the attitude she held during the war and for the support she extended to the Axis elements. His allegations had a great effect in North American public opinion. When the Russian request was debated in a secret session of foreign ministers representing the Big Four and those of Brazil, Chile, and Mexico, Stettinius, after various attempts to free himself of the agreements undertaken at Chapultepec, accepted the position of Molotov on condition that a similar invitation be extended to Argentina.

In a bitter debate Molotov repeated his criticisms of our country but declared that he would support its admission only if the United States would invite the Polish government of Lublin in addition to the two Soviet republics. Meanwhile, as Welles relates it, in the Brazilian city of Sao Paulo—simultaneously with the San Francisco conference—Argentine and Soviet representatives were working out the bases for the establishment of diplomatic and commercial relations.

In the face of the joint opposition of the United States and Great Britain, Molotov desisted in his attempt to incorporate the government of Lublin, and in the meeting of the Executive Committee the American delegates voted for the admission of the two Soviet republics, and the Russian delegate for the admission of Argentina.

BLUE BOOK'S BLUES

With diplomatic recognition and admission to the United Nations, the Argentine Revolution had escaped the international isolation to which it had been submitted. Everything led to the supposition that relations with the United States had at last reached a certain understanding. Although the international problems appeared solved, there still remained pending the internal problem. The complicated Argentine political process, and the necessary institutional way out, which the Revolutionary government was seeking, would become, however, the causes of a new confrontation with the United States.

Farrell on February 9, 1945, confirmed that Argentina had already reached the phase of a preelectoral organization, which would finally lead the country to "constitutional normality." On May 18 the minister of the interior announced the end of the state of siege and the creation of an electoral tribunal. Also, autonomy was returned to the universities. At this stage Spruille Braden was named ambassador of the United States in Argentina.

The lines were extended. Halperin Donghi, with reason, points out that after having been attacked, the myths of liberal Argentina showed themselves endowed with an unexpected vigor. The progress of the war without doubt was encouraging them. They were reflected in the angry and impatient crowds, demanding the unconditional surrender of the Fascists. For them Fascism

was represented by the Revolutionary government and its political servants. It was soon clear that Ambassador Braden "whose
rude frankness surpassed in brutality even that of the military
officers who were governing," was directing this movement. Braden considered the restoration of democracy and the downfall
of the military government as the principal goal of his mission.
He was not content to support his objectives with orthodox
diplomatic measures. He took advantage of every occasion publicly to attack the government as authoritarian and Fascist. He
made trips to the interior during which he was triumphally
received in university centers, where he formulated unmistakable
encouragement to overthrow the government. In autumn 1945
he interfered with the military necessities. He persuaded Assistant Secretary Rockefeller to cancel a shipment of arms authorized by the Lend-Lease administration. On May 29, Washington
announced that no kind of military equipment would be sent
as long as Argentina did not comply with the obligations undertaken in the conference at Chapultapec.

On July 7, in the traditional fellowship dinner of the armed
forces, Farrell, after denying the existence of divisions within the
army, announced a call for elections in February of the following year. Six days later, Labor groups in the Capital began the
presidential campaign of Perón. And on July 24 a Radical sector
issued a public manifesto inviting Perón to be their candidate.

In August Braden was named assistant secretary of state for
Latin American affairs. In an interview just before his departure for Washington, he told the press that there would be no
changes in his policy and that, on the contrary, his new position
would offer him greater possibilities for carrying it out. He also
said that official relations would depend upon future events from
which it was deduced that definitely they would depend upon
the results of the elections.

On October 9 the entire country was jolted with the news of
Perón's resignation from the three positions he was simultane-

ously fulfilling. In farewell, he addressed the public by radio and took advantage of the occasion to accuse Braden of interfering in the internal affairs of Argentina and of inciting rebellion. On October 12 Perón was arrested, and Farrell gave Juan Alvarez, the attorney general of the nation, the task of forming a new Cabinet.

Marches, countermarches, delay, and sluggishness characterized the new and ephemeral masters of the situation. On October 17 Perón victoriously returned to power and, for extra measure, with a myth. On October 22 free elections guaranteed by the army were promised, and on October 31 it was permitted that political parties begin their activities. Two broad coalitions were formed. One, made up of the traditional parties (Radicals, Socialists, Progressive Democrats, and Communists) adopted the name of *Unión Democrática*. The other had grouped around the figure of Perón the Radical nuclei, the nationalists, several Conservative sectors, the nacent labor organization, the army, and the Church.

Meanwhile from Washington, Braden continued his attacks against Perón, whom he considered a threat to the peace and security of the continent. Fifteen days before the elections, February 11, 1946, he decided to employ a supreme weapon which he considered infallible. He delivered to the representatives of the other American countries a memorandum, known as the "Blue Book," though entitled "Consultation Among the American Republics with Respect to the Argentine Situation." The Blue Book was based on information provided by the Allied Intelligence Services, as well as on documents captured from the Germans. There appeared in it lists of former agents of Germany, and the detailed activities of the Argentine government in favor of the Axis and against the security and peace of the hemisphere. Perón was singled out as the principal collaborator.

Braden's open intervention gave the candidate the backing that he needed at the moment. To present Perón as the champion of Argentine sovereignty was the sole objective of the Perónist strategy in the last days of the electoral campaign. According to such propaganda, the Argentines would have to choose on election day between Braden or Perón. On February 24, 1946, the candidate not favored by the United States was chosen as President. Welles, the tireless and bitter critic, comments:

> As a result of the policy that the United States had pursued toward Argentina during the preceding two and a half years, this country had received at the hands of the Argentine people the worst diplomatic defeat it ever sustained in the Western Hemisphere and had suffered a loss of influence and of prestige in South America that will not be forgotten for many years to come.

6: THE "THIRD POSITION"

AFTER FEBRUARY

In the February 1946 elections Perón had obtained a strong advantage, which permitted him without any difficulty to control the internal situation. But his electoral victory also signified a victory over the policy of pressure from North America and, therefore, the visible increase of his prestige within the Latin American sphere. Now his goal was turned toward finding a formula of getting along with the United States, that is, with the first power of the world, the winner of the war. It became a question then of consolidating the conquests achieved—among them, the prestige obtained as the champion of anti-Yankeeism in the continent—by means of a *modus vivendi* that would not alter them. In order to obtain it, the Perónist strategy would only review the old technique of the Conservative governments and of the June Revolution itself: to contain Washington's pressure or that of the inter-American system by gaining support from extrahemispheric countries. This support could be sought either in the traditional links with England or in the relations of the new Communist bloc. But, for the moment, the most urgent matter for Perón was to conclude the settlement with the United States. The opportunity would arise with the negotiations for organizing hemispheric defense. In accordance with Resolution VIII of the Act of Chapultepec, it had been established that the American states would agree to a treaty for the purpose of preventing and repressing threats and acts of aggression against any one of them. For this a meeting was scheduled in Rio de Janeiro beginning October 20, 1945. However, two weeks before the conference, Acting Secretary of State Acheson announced to the press that the North American government had approached the Brazilian Foreign Ministry with a request to postpone it. A cable from Reuters dated October 20, which was published in La Prensa, pointed out the purpose of the postponement: "The United States does not consider that it is possible to negotiate or to sign a treaty of military assistance with the present regime in Argentina."

This surprising North American decision—which displeased the other countries because, with the exception of Brazil, they had not been consulted beforehand—also had its repercussions in the United States Senate. The October 22 session, for the purpose of ratifying Braden's nomination as assistant secretary of state for Latin American affairs, gave various senators an opportunity to discuss the postponement of the Rio Conference, its causes, and its consequences. From the debate it came out that the idea of postponing the conference was recommended by Braden and approved by Acheson. Senator Robert LaFollette complained that both officials were acting precipitously without first consulting the Senate and the Pan American Union, and he raised some doubt as to the reliability of Braden's information about Argentina.

Toynbee says that Braden was counting on reaching an agreement with the other Latin American countries, excluding Argentina. But his efforts were frustrated by the opposition of these countries toward concluding an agreement under such conditions.

The electoral triumph of Perón modified even the intransigent line of Braden himself, who on March 27, 1946, with the official results of the election just certified, manifested that relations with Argentina would automatically continue in the new Buenos Aires government and that, unilaterally, sanctions would not be applied to the Perón regime. On the contrary, it would first be necessary to seek the advice and opinion of the other American nations and of some of the European nations. The results of these consultations were shown in the attitude of the Department of State and its memorandum of April 1:

> A new constitutional government will soon be inaugurated in Argentina. The Government of the United States feels it expresses the sentiments of all its sister governments in declaring its fervent hope that when the newly elected government takes office and its congress meets, it will give prompt implementation by positive acts to its solemn commitments under the Inter-American system, in particular those undertaken in the Final Act of the Inter-American Conference on the Problems of War and Peace. These undertakings are plain and unequivocal. They require the elimination from this Hemisphere of Axis influences which have threatened the security of the inter-American system.
>
> Were such unequivocal and sustained performance to ensue, the road would then be open to that "complete unity of the peoples of America," and the negotiation and signature of a Mutual Assistance Pact. But there must be deeds and not merely promises.

Perón was inaugurated June 4, 1946. That day in his first message to Congress he expressed his opinion about the new international obligations of the postwar period:

> . . . it is necessary to keep in mind that when international decisions exceed the general framework of the constitutional provisions, the people can choose between not validating the excesses which have been incurred or resorting to the reform of the Constitution. And on this delicate point—where the new-world conceptions of political and economic organization for the future, resting on the Acts of Mexico and San Francisco, converge or conflict with the traditional manner as established in our Great Charter—I will need the intelligence and the patriotism of the Honorable Members of Congress

in order to establish the certain definition of what best suits the Republic.

Without many scruples Perón hastened to establish diplomatic relations with the Soviet Union, and without waiting for the decision of Congress—manifested later in August—he received officially a special ambassador on June 6. During the war this gesture would have lacked any significance, because then the relations among the Allies were cordial. But successive crises had sharpened the separation between East and West, and the possibility of a war between the Soviet Union and the United States was already being discussed. This was the moment chosen by Perón to recognize Moscow and to broaden in some way his base for negotiation with the United States. Meanwhile, the lack of arms, examined above in Chapter IV, had found no final solution, in spite of the fact that the government made some important acquisitions in Great Britain. Immediately after assuming power in June 1946, Perón sent General von der Becke to the United States with the purpose of obtaining any kind of modern weapons for the Argentine army. The emissary talked with Acheson and Braden on June 18. An innocuous communiqué concealed the breakdown of the mission, according to the *New York Herald Tribune*. The North Americans would deliver weapons to the Argentine government only when the latter would comply with the obligations undertaken at Chapultapec.

Argentina could not elude them any longer. As a preannouncement of a conciliatory attitude, Perón on August 1 formulated some sensational declarations to a representative of the United Press:

> . . . we all know that there exists potentially the danger of other conflicts and if, unfortunately, the statesmen of the world cannot prevent them and, in the case of their materializing, Argentina would be found on the side of the United States and the other American nations.

He denied that he would seek the formation of a Latin American bloc as a counterweight to the United States, and he insisted thus:

> Argentina is a part of the American continent and inevitably will join the United States and the other nations of the American continent in any future conflict.

These declarations aroused favorable comments from the Department of State and from the Senate of the United States, from the President of Mexico, from the Uruguayan foreign minister, Eduardo Rodríguez Larreta (who boasted "This is a great triumph on which we must congratulate ourselves warmly") and in the American and European press.

Toward the end of June, Perón had sent the Chapultapec and San Francisco agreements to Congress. The Senate approved them unanimously with only a single speech, that of Diego Luis Molinari, whose text was regarded as the opinion of the President of the Republic himself. In the streets manifestations from the extreme nationalists condemned the treaties, accused Perón of treason, and clamored aloud for sovereignty. Foreign Minister Bramuglia, on August 21, delivered an address by radio in order to calm down the opinion.

> Argentine sovereignty has not been touched—or compromised. The charter of the United Nations and the Act of the Conference of Mexico do not have this force, and if the latter does not have specifications of a time limit, it is because there is no time limit. Thus it is known and understood by the states which have adhered to the spirit of the deliberations that best reflect hemispheric thought in its redeeming unity. . . . in no part of the Act of Chapultapec, in none of its declarations, recommendations or resolutions, is there advertence to the possibility of a centralized government, formed by the concurrence of the American governments either around the country considered strongest or around the country considered weakest.

In the Chamber of Deputies the matter did not turn out to be so easy. And, unexpectedly, the Peronist majority of the Commission on Foreign Affairs and Worship (Díaz de Vivar, Palacio, Antille, and Iturraspe) recommended, with the approval of the Senate, a reservation of the "rights and attributions inherent in Argentine sovereignty, and which by virtue of the National Constitution can only be exercised by the powers of the State in conformity with the laws that govern their exercise." For their part, the Radical minority (Candioti and Sanmartino) proposed approval, but they also inclined toward approval of the four interpretive clauses of the Act of Chapultapec and the Charter of the United Nations, although suggesting reforms that recalled Yrigoyen's objections to the League of Nations. Both proposals were rejected, and the approval originating from the Senate was accepted. The Radical contingent, after an intervention from Balbín, abstained from voting; seven deputies then separated themselves from the Peronist majority and voted against.

Now the Argentine government sought to gather the fruits of its good conduct. Bramuglia then stated publicly:

> The parliamentary approval which the Senate and the Chamber of Deputies of the Nation have given to the United Nations Charter and the Final Act of the Inter-American Conference on Problems of War and Peace defines the international policy of Argentina and justifies the constant and permanent claims of the country with regard to the appraisal and efficacy of its conduct for participating in the play of continental and universal interests.

There could not be a clearer allusion to the suspended Rio de Janeiro meeting.

The steps taken by Argentina still did not satisfy the Department of State, although powerful influences were moving evermore in our favor. The Pentagon also wanted an arrangement to standardize military equipment for all of America by means of exchange in some countries of obsolete armaments for modern weapons. Economic measures also favored the end of the conflict, and in the Senate voices of censure were heard against the unreasonable demands made upon Argentina. Furthermore, the discord between Braden and the ambassador in Buenos Aires, Messersmith, was already a public scandal. On January 8, 1947, Byrnes resigned as secretary of state and General Marshall took his place. The pending difficulties with the Argentine government were reduced to the existence of Nazi businesses, schools, and spies within the national territory. In order to mitigate the difficulties, the *de facto* government between November 1945 and February 1946 had dictated five decrees by which 73 Axis agents were deported. A sixth decree, this one from Perón, in November 1946 added to the list 52 more persons, among them the famous Harnisch, who was linked to the Hellmuth affair. On May 23, 1947, Bramuglia announced new deportations, stating that with these measures the government believed it had eliminated all the spies who were compromising continental security, and thus fulfillment was being given to the international obligations undertaken by the country at Chapultapec. With regard to the business enterprises, Decree 1,921, of January 24, 1947, ordered the acquisition in bloc of the goods and property of the nationals of Japan and Germany. In the text there is allusion to Resolutions XVIII and XIX of the Act of Chapultapec by virtue of which Argentina had contracted the obligation to liquidate said property.

On June 3, 1947, after a conversation of President Truman with Ambassador Ivanissevich, the White House announced the change of North American position. The official communiqué said:

> The Argentine Ambassador, who has just returned from Argentina, reviewed with the President and the Secretary of State the steps which his Government has taken and is con-

tinuing to take in fulfillment of its commitments undertaken in the final act of the Inter-American Conference on Problems of War and Peace. He expressed the view of his Government that no obstacle remained to discussions looking toward the treaty of mutual assistance contemplated by the Act of Chapultapec. The President indicated his willingness to renew the consultations with the governments of the other American republics initiated by the United States memorandum of April 1, 1946, on this subject.

The declaration only emphasized the new disposition in Washington, although diplomatic commentators discerned something more. A week before Truman had asked the United States Congress for a law that would authorize the supplying of modern-type weapons to the countries of Latin America.

Marshall and Atcheson attended the above mentioned interview, but Braden's absence was noted. Nor was he advised of Truman's declaration until it was published. With a certain symmetry, recovery was achieved from the surprising postponement of October 3, 1945. Braden did not resist this change, and two days later he resigned his post.

THE RIO TREATY

After this long transaction, Argentina arrived at the Rio conference with a power of negotiation visibly reduced. She was not in the position to reassume her typical defiant attitude in the continental harmony, or to jeopardize the costly reconciliation with the United States. The Inter-American Conference for the Maintenance of Continental Peace and Security met from August 15 until September 2, 1947. Foreign Minister Bramuglia headed our delegation, and the others were Enrique V. Corominas, Pascual La Rosa, Roberto Ares, Oscar Ivanissevich, and Nicolás Accame.

The circumstantial Argentine weakness was placed in evidence during the discussion of the central point of the meeting—the majority necessary for the functioning of the treaty. Leaving for Rio, Bramuglia had declared to the press that his delegation would maintain the unvariable Argentine criterion of unanimity. But the delegation was the only one to sustain it and had to abandon it very soon. Already on August 17, two days after the opening of the conference, it accepted the criterion of two-thirds. The article in question—Number 17—was finally stated as follows: "The Organ of Consultation shall take its decisions by a vote of two-thirds of the Signatory States which have ratified the treaty."

Up to now Argentina had always successfully defended the principle of unanimity in fundamental questions, for it included a veto power. This principle had been the norm of the decisions of the inter-American system, with the exception of questions of procedure. As was seen in the third consultation meeting (Rio, 1942), Welles had to sacrifice various projects in order to obtain the Argentine vote and with it the indispensable unanimity.

Submission to what was resolved by the majority of the conference was later explained by Perón in his message to Congress when he sought ratification:

> The Argentine delegation maintained the criterion that unanimity, which permitted all the countries to line up without reservations in any decision, was the ideal which the treaty ought to follow. Among the various points of view maintained by the attending delegations, a transactional solution was achieved consisting in that the various measures contained in Article 8 would be adopted by vote of two-thirds of the signatory states ratifying the treaty, with the single exception that no state would be obliged to employ armed force without its consent.

The last words reproduce almost textually Article 20. Although this last compensation was grasped at, Argentina renounced what had been for her a traditional posture of independent policy with respect to the inter-American system and, in a certain manner, with respect to the United States.

In spite of this concession, our country struggled to exclude from the force of the treaty conflicts between American countries and to limit it entirely to extrahemispheric aggression. The United States reacted strongly against this attempt, and in the discussions of the commission Senator Vandenberg maintained that with the adoption of this criterion the treaty would be converted into an "armed alliance against the rest of the world," and that "thus conceived it would cease to be an expression of a regional system." For him the "inter-American aggression constitutes a much greater offense than extrahemispheric."*

In this area Argentina obtained only what was called "peaceful consultation," a system which consisted in exhausting the means of peaceful solution before collectively intervening in inter-American conflicts (Article 7).

Also, the Argentine delegation sought to exclude from the scope of the treaty any stipulation that might bind the nations of the continent in the case of an attack on a territory under American jurisdiction, but situated outside the zone delineated in the treaty as the Security Zone. Thus was repeated the thesis of Ruiz Guiñazú when in 1942 he considered the attack on Pearl Harbor as an aggression outside America. This was not accepted by the United States, and a transactional solution was reached at the suggestion of Mexico. According to this, the extracontinental juridiction of the American states had to be "effective."

The Argentine government boasted about having obtained the inclusion in the pact of the nonautomatic principle. In the above cited message to Congress, Perón maintained that "in accordance with the orientation sustained in principal degree by the Argentine delegation, the treaty contains no automatic obli-

* The words of Senator Vandenberg are translated from Argentine newspaper accounts.

gations." In effect, a previous stage was required—the meeting of the organ of consultation—so that the dispositions might be binding.

At the same time the Argentine delegation succeeded in suppressing from Article 6 the concept of "threat of aggression," though this was included in the United Nations Charter, because the Argentines maintained that in this way one could reach a judgment about the subjective elements in the politics of the signatory countries and even intervention in internal matters of the states. On the other hand, there was assurance that only a certain and objective fact could form part of the material of discussion in the meeting of consultation.

Instructions imparted to our delegation singled out, as a primordial end to obtain, that the treaty should contain a clause for denunciation.

The message from the executive branch warned:

> No state has the right to tie itself up in perpetuity and, although the principle of solidarity forms an essential part of the American institutions, a treaty that might regulate the forms of activity of this solidarity ought to have a flexibility that would include—if the case should require it—even unilateral denunciation.

Argentine concern was made real in Article 25.

In the elaboration of the military pact of Rio, as Smith notes, our delegation did not fall back on the traditional obstructionist role of the Argentine representatives to inter-American conferences. The Peronist representation consummated the return of Argentina to the hemispheric meetings, displaying an attitude of relative cooperation with the United States. For the moment it could not be any other way.

THE ECONOMIC WAR

Although in the political aspect a certain understanding had been achieved with the United States, this laborious truce would prove to be ephemeral, and the next battle would break out in the economic field.

The Perón government wanted to carry out a fundamental reform of economic policy, already fostered by certain measures of the *de facto* government that were ratified and improved by its constitutional successor. In synthesis the reform included the nationalization of the Central Bank and therefore of the whole credit system, the management of the kinds of exchange, and the monopoly of foreign commerce.

Then came the establishment of the Argentine Institute for the Promotion of Interchange (IAPI), which originally was the only buyer of grain and vegetable oils at the prices fixed in advance by the government, and which was charged with the placing of these commodities in the foreign market. In time, IAPI achieved the centralization of the acquisition of raw materials and capital goods in those markets. It was used, for example, as means to buy the British and French railways, the telephone, vessels for the merchant fleet, and even for the construction of the pipe line from Comodoro Rivadavia.

The monopoly of foreign commerce achieved by means of IAPI was one of the dogmas of Peronism: it was incorporated in one of the clauses of the Constitution of 1949, the famous Article 40, which places the importation and exportation in the hands of the State, according to whatever limitations and control the law may determine. As a consequence of this, the channels of foreign commerce also had to be changed. Peronism supplanted the type of bilateral relations the country had maintained until then, a system based on tariff reductions and customs exemptions by a "strict bilateralism" as much in the economic order as in the financial.

The statism of the government, begun in 1946, responded to an old Argentine ideological tendency which had already started with the Conservative governments and which had received a strong impulse from nationalist thought. But in this instant it was not achieved within the international context that followed the 1930 crisis; now the situation of the country was not so afflicted as to justify the intensification of the interventionist measures; on the contrary, the world was going rapidly toward liberation from restrictions and toward multilateralism.

Even during the war, in July 1944, the Allied nations met in Bretton Woods, where they concluded agreements tending to the stabilization of exchange, the proscription of deficit liquidation, the reactivation of trade and the avoiding of oscillation in the exchange systems. For these purposes the International Bank for Reconstruction and Development and the International Monetary Fund were established.

To these early attempts at liberation of foreign trade, the *de facto* government had adhered by means of Decree 3,185 (January 31, 1946) one of whose considerations recognized "that in spite of restrictions on its rights, which in financial matters these agreements presuppose, the government esteems that their renunciation is a just tribute to harmony and wholesome cooperation among the peoples of the international community."

The constitutional government, in accordance with established practice, sent the Congress this decree among others for its ratification and obtained the corresponding sanction of the Senate. But when came the Deputies' turn, at the insistence of the Radical minority in the Commission on Decrees, the decree was not approved. Shortly afterward the executive branch sent a new message advising that the decree not be ratified, since in its judgment these ". . . organisms, so long as they conserve their present structure, are not in condition to comply with the ends of international financial reorganization for which they were created. . . ."

The second attempt at reorganization of world commerce was in 1945, the so-called Clayton Plan for the expansion of commerce and employment. It was based on six principles: increase in foreign trade; freedom of private initiative; multilateral trade; elimination of preferences; stable commercial policy; and international cooperation. This plan was the base for negotiations that lasted more than two years, and had culminated in the United Nations Conference on Trade and Employment held in Havana between November 21, 1947, and March 29, 1948. The Argentine delegation was headed by Senator Diego Luis Molinari, who tried to capitalize on the sentiments of the countries of Latin America when he denounced the North American proposal for reduction in customs barriers as an attempt to hold back the industrialization of those countries in order to maintain them in colonial servitude.

His voice prevailed in a conference oriented toward freedom of trade, because in upholding the position of the Argentine government he maintained a statist thesis at all costs:

> We believe that economic government and political government cannot be in distinct and diverse hands, but that in the integral conception of democracy the government of the economic and of the political belong to one and the same power. . . . There could be no human force capable of turning us from these directions today except a cataclysm for the world and for my country, and we will not renounce the economic control of our people and of our nation.

Finally, when the time came to sign the Havana charter, Argentina—together with Poland—preferred to abstain.

In this conference, Molinari was conscious of the necessity to answer the frequent accusation that Argentina in her manner of allotting products was speculating with the hunger of peoples. He recalled the donations, the loans at low interest made by our country. But he went beyond that when, in the middle of December 1947, he declared to the press that Argentina could send to European countries the equivalent of five billion dollars as an aid to the Marshall Plan. The following day, Foreign Minister Bramuglia hastened to clarify this from Buenos Aires. He said that Molinari was referring to an optimistic assessment of our exports and that, therefore, his offer did not allude to any real money. The editorial in the *New York Times*, December 19, 1947, was even more severe: it judged Molinari's declaration as an example of Argentine error in looking at the Marshall Plan as a commercial enterprise. It also criticized the country's attitude that selling food to nations in need was a form of aid.

The Marshall Plan

These verbal excesses were already announcing the problem of Argentina regarding the Marshall Plan.

The difficult economic situation of the European countries at the close of the war moved the United States to work out a plan destined to reconstruct the devastated economies of the Old World. The policy repeated the gesture of gift or donation extended during the war under the Lend-Lease Act. United States would supply, in the form of loans or gifts, the equipment, capital, raw materials, and food that the European countries needed. The essence of this operation was political and not economic, because in addition to the benefits that certainly would revert to the United States, its principal goal was to drive the communist danger from a Europe enmeshed in a low standard of life.

The Plan had its origin in a speech given by Secretary of State General George Marshall at Harvard University June 5, 1947, and was approved by the European countries—except those of the Soviet orbit that rejected it—in a meeting at Paris the end of December. After extended consideration, the North American Congress approved the Foreign Assistance Act, better known as "The Marshall Plan," which according to its title sought to "promote world peace and the general welfare, national interest, and foreign policy of the United States through economic, financial, and other measures necessary to the maintenance of conditions abroad in which free institutions may survive and consistent with the maintenance of the strength and stability of the United States."

In Argentina the Plan aroused great hopes. The country possessed, at that time, a considerable surplus of raw materials that could be contributed on a grand scale toward the ends of the undertaking through purchase by the European nations helped by the United States. But at the same time, Argentina was suffering a severe dollar shortage. The program of nationalization, the redemption of the public debt and the acquisitions carried out by IAPI had consumed a good part of the reserves accumulated during the war. On the other hand, trade with the United States showed a pronounced imbalance against our country. In fact, if in 1946 our exports reached 596 million pesos and imports 665 million, the following year imports reached 2.431 millions against only 547 of Argentine exports. Evidently the Marshall Plan could offer a solution to so serious a problem.

However, Argentina constructed a rigid policy regarding this opportunity. As has already been explained, the IAPI monopolized foreign commerce and thus sought to intervene with greater weight in world trade. It bought Argentine products at a low price in order to then attempt selling them at higher prices than those reached in the international market. For example, in June 1948, the price of wheat in the United States was in their dollars 2.50 a bushel, while the IAPI was trying to sell wheat at 4.86 dollars. This policy of high prices conflcted with an expressed norm of the Marshall Plan (Section 112 of the law), by which purchases abroad of products that could be obtained at lower prices in the United States were not permitted. The policy also aroused bitter criticism in North American opinion. Thus, the *Washington Post*, October 31, 1947, considered the Argentine transactions as a kind of international black market in wheat, putting the squeeze on nations whose dollar reserves were practically exhausted. Meanwhile, the Economic Cooperation Administration (ECA), the agency charged with administering the Marshall Plan, advised Argentina to adjust to world prices in order to participate in the plan as a source of supply.

The Peronist interpretation justified the price level then required by the high quotation of the industrial products, which in turn our country had to acquire. It argued that the Argentine government had offered its production at so called world prices as long as indispensable materials at current prices in the United States could be guaranteed, since this interpretation sustained that these prices were artificially raised against Argentina. Such was the tenor of the conversations between Miguel Miranda and North American Ambassador James Bruce in November 1947.

Under another aspect, it was inevitable that the IAPI system would enter into conflict with North American policy of liberalizing world trade. Bruce himself, who made some effort in his country in the hope of avoiding Argentina's remaining isolated from economic reactivation, pointed out that

> . . . the best hope of Argentina to continue its commercial prosperity rests more on reentry into the world of free initiative and the competition of private enterprise than on the prices fixed by governmental decision.*

The most delicate point, however, was the freezing of the funds due from earnings on North American investments in Argentina. The government's position was tersely defined by Miranda who stated in a press interview that there could be no expectation of dividends until Argentina had the dollars. The problem moved *Time* magazine to state (September 19, 1948) that Ambassador Bruce had had not a few headaches in Buenos Aires in consequence of the suppression of payment on North American investments in that country and of the rigid norms imposed against North American capital in Argentine business.

---

* Argentine newspapers are given as the source of the quote, which is translated here from the authors' Spanish citation.

The magazine added that ECA had advised Bruce that the agency would not spend a single cent of United States taxpayers' money in Argentina until the Perón government promised categorically to sell its products at world market prices and to renew payment on North American investments in Argentina.

In spite of these unfavorable signs Miranda maintained, "If people need to eat, as I believe they do, then they will have to obtain dollars and bring them here to buy food from us." For the clique that was running our economy then was absolutely convinced that the Argentine market could dominate the situation. This certainty was to be lost.

The circumstances enumerated combined with good harvests in the United States and in Europe itself let that country disregard Argentina in its program of European rehabilitation. Important ECA bids were assigned to competing markets and our country had no access to our traditional markets. This situation led Perón to state:

> The Marshall Plan was a real scourge for the Latin American economy. It eliminated every possibility of surpluses through the genuine "dumping" carried on by the United States. This practice constituted for countries like ours a true aggression against the economy, and this provoked great difficulties in 1948.

The Marshall Plan, then, was upsetting our trade with Europe. There was no relief in sight for our painful dollar shortage. Argentina had to attempt a solution, no matter how dangerous, of these problems. It was necessary to find an ally who in economics would subscribe to similar principles (statism and bilateralism) and who in politics would oppose the United States— something to fall back on in case of a major confrontation with the latter country. At this point Peronism again failed to show any innovation with respect to its predecessor governments; the chosen ally was to be socialist Great Britain.

PERÓN AND THE BRITISH

The war effort had obliged England to liquidate almost the totality of her overseas investments. The government had requisitioned the latter from private owners to realize them in the United States, Canada, and the other Dominions. Thus Britain had to renounce her traditional economic system based on income received from abroad. At the end of the war it had changed from a creditor nation to the biggest debtor nation of the world, and the possibility of achieving a favorable balance of payments appeared remote indeed. This situation came to a head at the same time as the electoral victory of the Labour Party and Labour's program of nationalization and state intervention began to be carried into practice. In 1946 the banking system, the coal industry, and civil aviation were all nationalized. In the following year so were the transportation and electric power enterprises, and in 1948 the gas industry. The turn for iron and steel came in 1949, and there was not much more delay for medicine and the petroleum companies.

Immediately after the cessation of hostilities with the sudden surrender of Japan, Britain ceased to receive aid under Lend-Lease. On August 21, 1945, President Truman notified the beneficiary governments that such aid would be halted at once. The desperate situation of the British, however, moved both countries to undertake negotiations toward a solution of the situation. The negotiations were difficult and lengthy. Finally, on December 6, an agreement was reached for a loan in amount of 4 billion dollars with repayment over a period of 50 years at an interest rate of 2 per cent.

In exchange for so favorable a loan, certain conditions were imposed on Britain. In accordance with the policy of liberalizing world trade, the United States required the dissolution of the "sterling bloc" within one year after the delivery of the funds. All existing restrictions that hindered the exchange of pounds in ordinary transactions would have to be eliminated. Also with the loan came an end to the separation between the dollar and the sterling zones—the two zones between which international trade was divided, as though between two walled-off monopolies, on account of the inconvertibility of British money. In regard to sterling balances accumulated during the war in London in favor of the supplying countries, the United Kingdom obligated itself to reach agreements with the creditors as quickly as possible, although the releasing and convertibility of these balances were not specifically provided for in the agreement with the United States. Britain also consented to support United States proposals for a conference on trade and employment (Havana, 1947–1948) and to adhere to the Bretton Woods Pacts.

The Miranda-Eady Agreement

It was this exhausted and socialist Britain that the Perón government approached in search of support. A month after the inauguration the government cordially received a British mission headed by Sir Wilfred Eady. Long drawn-out negotiations ended in the convention of September 17, 1946, signed by the British envoy and Miguel Miranda. The negotiations were drawn out because Great Britain sought to use the results as a pilot convention to be extended to other creditor nations, India, Egypt, and others. As Cafiero concedes, it cost the Argentine government something to win some progress with great difficulty and at the same time to budge the British who were anxious not to establish any precedents that other countries with blocked pounds could utilize.

According to the terms of the Anglo-American agreement of December 1945, Great Britain now agreed that all the pounds which in the future Argentina might receive would be "freely disposable for the payment of current transactions in any place." It recognized, in this way, the convertibility of the pound, money which could be used as a means of payment in other markets.

With respect to the blocked pounds, the new agreement did not respect the Anglo-American Treaty of 1945. In fact, almost all the balance in London remained frozen, except ten million pounds that were freed in order to transfer them to Brazil and five million annually over a period of four years for the payment of current transactions. The rest of the frozen balance, almost intact, would yield the moderate interest of one-half per cent freely available. In exchange, the Treaty admitted without limitations the employment of these balances for the repatriation of public debt in pounds and for the redemption of British investments in Argentina.

Another clause provided that ". . . if in any year the balance of payments with the sterling area should be unfavorable for Argentina, the latter will be able to dispose freely of its balances in pounds within the sterling area through imports equivalent to the deficit."

The following details will indicate that this clause, in view of the violation of the 1945 Anglo-American agreement, had aroused Washington's criticism.

With respect to meat, the British government obligated itself to buy our export quota for four years, except for a reserve for sale by the Argentine government in other markets of not more than 17 per cent in the first year and 22 per cent in the second.

Regarding the railroads, it was agreed to form a mixed society made up of British investors, with shares of a sum equal to the present value of the railroads, and of the Argentine State which would invest in the new society five hundred million pesos in cash for the purpose of modernizing the railroad system. The Argentine government reserved the right to acquire at any time after a reasonable notice at par value a part or the totality of the shares in the hands of whatever holder. At the same time, the government guaranteed the new society a net return of not less than 4 per cent annually. And, finally, the customs exemptions which would have terminated at an early date under the Mitre Law were renewed:

The Argentine government will exempt the new company from any and all national, provincial, and municipal taxes, present and future, and will at the same time exempt the new company from any and all customs duties, present and future, on the materials and articles for construction and exploitation which it may introduce into Argentina.

Business had not been brilliant for Argentina. *La Prensa*, August 19, 1946, commented with reason that the British mission had had a complete success, since in a single stroke the railroad companies resolved all the problems. The freeing of our balances in London was ridiculous. Great Britain in a world of need assured herself of the greater part of our export of meats. The railroads were nationalized only in name, but in reality we were returning to the regime of the guaranteed railroads.

The signing of the Miranda-Eady Agreement was censured by the United States Secretary of Treasury John Snyder in correspondence which he maintained with his British colleague, Hugh Dalton, between October 31, 1946, and January 7, 1947. He took a very firm stand on the above cited clause from the Treaty, according to which, if the balance of payments with the sterling area was unfavorable for Argentina, this country could freely dispose of its balances in pounds within the same area by an importation equivalent to the deficit. Thus there was a violation of the obligation to establish the convertibility of the pound— an obligation assumed by England in her agreement with the United States in 1945. To justify his government, Dalton could not find anything better than to reply that the Anglo-Argentine commerce never produced a deficit against the traditional supplier of England. This specious argument did not convince Snyder, who indicated to the British minister that this type of clause could destroy the effect of the Anglo-American Treaty of 1945.

Railroads, Pounds, and Arms

The conjecture can be admitted that the North American pressure may have been the reason why the Miranda-Eady Agreement never was put into practice. At least, with regard to the railroads, not even the first necessary steps were undertaken to form the mixed society and, unexpectedly, only four months after the signing of the Agreement, February 2, 1947, announcement was made of the direct purchase of the English railroads by the Argentine government. In fact, on February 13, a new agreement was signed by Miguel Miranda, as president of the IAPI, and the British enterprises represented by Sir Montague Eddy. According to the agreement, the railroad system and its accessory establishments were acquired for a sum of 2,482.5 million pesos (150 million pounds), exempt from all tax. Nothing, however, was said about the form of payment that was determined early in the following year, as will be noted. In the drafting and signing of this treaty, the minister of finance and the minister of public works had no part at all—nor had the minister of foreign affairs, who limited himself to sending a note ratifying it. For the sake of appearances, Article 16 contained this guarantee:

> Both parties desire to make expressly clear that the present contract is the result of the negotiations, the initial bases of which were decided in the agreement of September 17, 1946 . . . and which was authorized with the knowledge of the government of the United Kingdom for the purpose of giving to that agreement the new form, which under the present circumstances has been considered the most convenient for the Argentine government.

Hardly six months had passed since Perón, in an interview with United Press representative A. L. Bradford, had indicated scant interest in the purchase of the British railroads, which he qualified as "old iron" (La Prensa, August 2, 1946). Another capital point of the Miranda-Eady Agreement remained fruitless in effect. Everything established on the convertibility of the pounds Argentina might obtain in her trade after the signing of said agreement, as well as the minimum part disposable from the former balances in London, would become a dead letter by the unilateral decision of the British on August 20, 1947, which declared the pound to be again inconvertible. It will be remembered that in the Anglo-American agreement of 1945, Great Britain had obligated herself to convert her money to any other without any limitation. Nevertheless, the rapid evaporation of dollar reserves led her, after a consultation with the United States, to decree the inconvertibility. To our scarcity of North American exchange, treated above under the Marshall Plan, were now added these restrictions on the pound, which made even more difficult the obtaining of dollars, which were indispensable for Argentina.

Meanwhile, the Perón government was undertaking important acquisition of weapons in England. Between January and October 1947, for example, it invested 2,600,000 pounds in the purchase of airplanes, the third part of the total of the British sales during this period (Brazil had bought a value of 83,000 pounds, and Chile only 3,000). These arguments, in addition to previous purchases from the same origin, were in response to the lack of agreement with the United States on the material. Toward the end of 1947 Lieutenant General Willis L. Crittenberger took advantage of an official visit to Argentina to undertake negotiations for the provisioning of arms and military materials. Only a reduced quantity was made certain. The New York Herald Tribune, December 1, 1947, noted that the North American army was interested in equipping the Argentine air force and in establishing meteorological stations in the extreme south—but that everything had become complicated with the procurement of English fighters and bombers, inasmuch as the United States would have to compete with Great Britain in the standardization of arms in the hemisphere.

The Andes Agreement

Although the purchase of the British railroads for the sum of 150 million pounds had been formalized in February 1947, an agreement was still lacking as to the payment for them. There also remained pending the question of the Argentine balances in London on account of the decreed inconvertibility. The agreement of February 18, 1948, called "Andes" referred to both questions.

As it was foreseen, the old credit balances in London were not used for the payment of the railroads. It was agreed to apply the value of Argentine exports of 1948 along with the balances pending delivery of the contracts still in effect. By means of a financial play, Great Britain advanced to Argentina the value of the products that the latter would send to her, and this advance would be transferred to the British railroad enterprises. In fact, England advanced 100 million pounds for the Argentine 1948 export and 10 million more for the greatest possible costs; finally, the remaining 40 million were completed with the balance in Argentina's favor when in August 1947 the inconvertibility of the pound was decreed. For the nationalization of the railroads, then, there was no recourse to the balances that had been blocked in Great Britain during the war.

These were finally freed, but without making them convertible. They were to be applied only to commercial transactions carried out entirely within the sterling area. For them the British continued to pay us the annual one-half per cent interest.

Other provisions of the above treaty alluded to the purchase of 400,000 tons of meat and meat products; 20,000 of canned beef and mutton; and slightly more than 1,200,000 tons of corn, barley, linseed oil, fats, and tallow. Argentina on her part assumed the obligation of taking 2,500,000 cubic meters of petroleum products, a million tons of coal, 75,000 tons of steel, as well as various chemical products.

The Agreement took effect by means of exchange of notes on

February 19, 1948, without any intervention on the part of Congress.

The Complementing of Great Britain

The high-price policy followed by Argentina with respect to the program of purchases under the Marshall Plan had left her practically on the margin of this undertaking. In fact, until March 1949, in the sales from Latin America destined for the plan, Argentina occupied the last place with only 0.26 per cent of the total. Evidently the Marshall Plan brought no benefit to the country but, on the contrary, had deprived Argentina of her traditional buyers.

On the other hand, the inconvertibility of the pound, following the disposition of the British government in August 1947, upset the development of our foreign trade—not only with the United Kingdom, but also with those countries with which we had unfavorable balances, particularly the United States, which before had been paid in substantial part by the conversion of the surplus in sterling. This aggravated even more the chronic scarcity of dollars and prevented our ready acquisition of the indispensable goods from abroad.

The new economic team that replaced Miranda, in order to raise to the maximum our foreign trade in spite of the scarcity of dollars, had inaugurated a broad policy of bilateral conventions. It was sought to dispose of our exports and obtain the necessary goods and materials without having recourse to the North American money. In this sense, the agreement negotiated in 1949 with Great Britain would be not only the most important in our history, but also the model according to which numerous treaties with other countries would be adjusted. "But when two economies are so admirably complementary as ours and the United Kingdom's, it is difficult not to find the basis that will permit the reaching of a commercial agreement of reciprocal interest.

. . ." Thus Roberto Ares, the minister of economy, declared with enthusiasm in the Chamber of Deputies.

But it was not only a decisive economic step, for it also implied a political act of the greatest transcendence. This complementarism with England permitted the Perón government to confront the United States on a more solid basis with due respect to extracontinental support. The old formula of Argentine diplomacy would come to life again under Peronism. The firm attitudes in Washington would always be paid for by condescending attitudes in London.

The importance of the treaty clearly issued from its sum 250 million pounds. It was the most remarkable treaty signed by Argentina and one of the greatest of the world. Its time limit was five years, although each year the respective governments reserved the right to renounce it. Its explicit end supported a growing interchange between both countries according to the bilateral scheme:

> Article 2: The contracting Governments will undertake major efforts to intensify business and financial transactions between the Argentine Republic and the United Kingdom in such a way that will permit the achievement over the period of the agreement of a balance of payments of pound sterling of the highest possible level.

The foreseen transactions duplicated the picture of the former agreement signed during the government of Perón: meats and cereals in exchange for fuel, iron, steel, chemical products, and some industrial articles. There existed, however, a discrimination: the prices of the Argentine products were fixed, although they could be readjusted annually; on the other hand, the English products would be quoted in accordance with the prices of world market, especially with regard to petroleum. As with the earlier balances, those resulting from this treaty would be inconvertible and could only be utilized for current operations within the sterling area. The North American government was not disinterested in this agreement; in a certain way, it was the principal one affected by its clauses, as Walter Lippmann recognized in *La Prensa*, June 25, 1949, when he noted that Argentina and Great Britain would exchange meat and petroleum under the proposed agreement, and that this exchange could exclude the petroleum of North American producers. But, Lippmann also pointed out, neither Argentina nor Great Britain were likely to have dollars to buy in the North American market anyway.

What disturbed Washington most before the signing was the possible rigidity of the treaty. Above all, an excessive duration and the unalterable character of the prices would have placed a discriminatory regime against United States products and her efforts toward the implantation of multilateralism. Before the Senate of the United States the director of ECA, Paul G. Hoffman, declared that this agency could exercise a great pressure to avoid the signing of a commercial pact like the Anglo-Argentine, and he threatened as an extreme measure the cancellation of aid to England [for the duration of the agreement] in order to support the protest of the Department of State (*Washington Post*, June 25, 1949). North American and English officials discussed the project, and to Washington must be attributed without doubt the clause of denunciation included in Article 1, as well as the annual revision of the prices of the products to be exchanged.

Once the agreement was signed, the Department of State issued a declaration which summed up its attitude toward it.

> During the course of the negotiations between the British and Argentine Governments which led to the adoption of the Trade and Payments Agreement, representatives of the Department of State engaged in a number of discussions with British and Argentine representatives regarding the proposed agreement. . . . On studying the final terms, the Department is gratified to observe that substantially more flexibility is

incorporated in its provisions than had at first been informally reported. . . .

The United States notes that the United Kingdom-Argentine arrangements provide for the right of termination . . . at the end of any year by either party, that prices contained in the meat contracts are subject to annual agreement by the parties, and that the export and import of other products, including petroleum products, depends upon the subsequent negotiations of buyers and sellers. The agreement by its terms may therefore be adapted to changing circumstances.

The United States is pleased to note the United Kingdom's reaffirmation of its basic objective of returning to convertibility and multilateralism and its disavowal of an intention to discriminate against the trade of third countries. The United States also notes that neither the United Kingdom nor Argentina is obliged by the terms of the agreement to purchase goods from the other at prices in excess of those available in other markets. . . .

The passage of time and, above all, the devaluation of the pound on August 19, 1949, changed the terms of the agreement, which resulted in successive readjustments by means of additional agreements, as was foreseen. Finally, in March 1955, a new agreement was signed with the innovation that the prices for meat were freed to be determined by the market. This corresponded to the new policy of liberation of the economy and multilateralism which was prevalent in England.

PERÓN AND PAN-AMERICANISM

The Chapultapec Conference in Resolution IX anticipated the military and institutional bases of the Pan-American system. In 1947 the Rio Treaty established the first. It remained for the Ninth Inter-American Conference to make real the juridical structure of the regional organism. The meeting, postponed from

1946, took place in the city of Bogotá March 30 to May 2, 1948 —interrupted for one week by the insurrection following the assassination of Jorge Eliecer Gaitán. Foreign Minister Bramuglia headed the Argentine delegation made up of Enrique V. Corominas, Pascual La Rosa, Pedro J. Vignale, Saverio S. Valente, Mariá E. Lopez Cabanillas de Ivanissevich, Roberto Ares, and Orlando Maroglio.

In this Conference Argentina did not take the attitude of collaboration she had shown the year before in Rio. On the contrary, she flaunted her traditional position against the development of the Pan-American system. The instructions to our delegation specified:

> 1. The charter of the Pan-American system must be structured in such form that it cannot presuppose the creation of a superstate.
>
> 2. It must contain only norms of juridical character with the political and military necessarily being eliminated. . . .
>
> 4. The Directive Council must not have political attributions.

This design was already manifest in the discussion of the name of the future entity. In its project, the Pan American Union had proposed the designation of "Constitutive Pact of the Inter-American System," and Brazil proposed that of "Pact of the Union of the American Nations." The former name was objectionable to the Argentine delegate La Rosa because of the word "constitutive," for in his judgment it overlooked the earlier efforts; he preferred the term "system" because of its reference to a collection of juridical norms and not to a new entity. For his part, Foreign Minister Bramuglia specified: "We have come to Bogotá to achieve an agreement of wills and not to create an organization and entity whose parts may be confused with the whole. As I am the Argentine Foreign Minister, I have to adjust myself to what the Constitution of my country provides. There it says that the national has preeminence over the international.

Furthermore at Chapultapec it was said that we would come here to consolidate a pact."

He foresaw that Argentina would formulate reservations if it were decided to accept as definition "union" or "association."

From this point of view our delegation was also opposed to collective action as the typical mark of the superstate, and it obtained the suppression of the following paragraph in the proposal for the charter: "The collective action provided in this pact or in the Charter of the United Nations does not constitute intervention." The logical consequence of its refusal to admit a superstate was to demand the suppression of Articles 35 and 36 of the project for the Pan American Union. As proposed, Article 35 stated that the Council takes cognizance "within the limits which this pact and the inter-American treaties and agreements establish of any matter that may affect the functioning and the ends of the inter-American system." Our delegation also proposed that the following be expressly added to the pact: "Functions of the Pan American Union and the Directive Council will not have a political character." Argentina did not have any success in its attempt to deprive the council completely of political faculties, but she succeeded in diminishing them, for the final draft read as follows:

> Article 50. The Council takes cognizance, within the limits of the present charter and of inter-American treaties and agreements, of any matter referred to it by the Inter-American Conference or the Meeting of Consultation of Ministers of Foreign Affairs.

In this way, the preponderant position of the Organ of Consultation and the Inter-American Conference within the regional system was strengthened and the latitude of the original definition reduced.

The instructions to our delegation prescribed in point 2 that military norms ought to be eliminated from the future charter.

In fulfilling their instructions, the Argentine representatives succeeded in severing from the Council of the Organization of American States the Inter-American Defense Board, which, according to the project, would constitute a specialized agency of the former. Also in accordance with the instructions (point 3) the delegation defended the independence of the Treaty of Reciprocal Assistance from the Organization of American States.

As in the year before at Rio, Argentina fought for a clause of denunciation to be included in the Charter. Instructions specified in point 8 that the pact "ought to contain clauses of (a) denunciation and (b) amendment with the previous agreement of the signatory states that have ratified it." The proposal was converted into Articles 111 and 112 of the final text.

The United States, Brazil, and Chile presented an energetic proposal to prevent and uproot from America all subversive activity of any totalitarianism, particularly the communist. To this, Bramuglia insisted that causes should be attacked before the effects, and that the ideas of social justice and democratic development should be taken into consideration. His insistence contained the threat of opposing "specific reservations." His motion became Resolution XXXII of the Conference. The foreign minister himself told the newspapermen:

> Regarding the communist question, I believe that they have taken into consideration the position which we manifested even before the Conference. We not only succeeded in having the fundamentals of the original proposal modified, but also we got into the text our formulation of the problem. Before fighting consequences, it is preferable to overcome the causes.

After a short trip to Canossa, Argentina was returning to her critical and challenging attitude with respect to the inter-American system.

THE KOREAN CRISIS

On June 25, 1950, communist troops from North Korea, on the pretext of uniting the peninsula, crossed the border and invaded South Korea. The United States decided immediately to intervene in the conflict. Two days later the Security Council of the United Nations decreed sanctions against the aggressor. With the whole world in agitation, the Argentine Congress on June 28 surprisingly ratified the Rio Treaty. The causes and consequences of this act will be examined later.

On June 30 Foreign Minister Hipólito Jesús Paz, in reply to the informative communications from the Security Council on its action in Korea, made manifest the adherence of our country to the Security Council's decision and her solidarity with the American republics. Furthermore, he instructed the ambassador in Washington to assure Secretary of State Acheson that "in the present circumstances the Argentine government has the pleasure of communicating that it supports with all its decisions the attitude of his government and the determinations which move it."

At the end of June the secretary general of the United Nations, Trigve Lie, sounded out the Argentine government on the possibility that our country might provide military aid and assistance in the Korean matter. The Foreign Ministry replied without any loss of time:

> In reply to your telegram of June 29 regarding the resolution of the Security Council adopted in the 474th meeting, I have the honour to inform you that the Argentine Government ratifies the communication sent to said Council and reiterates its decided support of that organization as a means of achieving effective and permanent peace.
>
> It reaffirms in this sense its will to comply, according to the measure of its possibilities, with the international pacts which it has signed.

Along the same lines, Perón, during the traditional fellow-ship dinner of the armed forces, dedicated a paragraph of his speech to Argentina's adherence:

> Therefore, this year of San Martín finds us Argentines on the way to full adherence and solidarity with the peoples of America—adherence not in the sense of submission with which Argentina, in opprobrious times, signed its obligations, but in the new and high sense of the free acts of a people that has achieved the fullness of its rights and of its dignity.

Again the secretary general of the United Nations addressed the Argentine government to inform it that the unified command had been entrusted to the United States and that, therefore, she would be in direct touch with Argentina to coordinate whatever aid could be extended. He also reported that the new Command had informed him of the urgent necessity for additional effective aid, and that in consequence the Security Council would be grateful to Argentina for considering the possibility of providing combat forces. The government did not delay in replying to the international organization in the following terms:

> In this respect, I take pleasure in expressing to you that the Argentine Government has taken due note of your communication and that in accordance with the purpose of fulfilling the obligations it has contracted as member of the United Nations, especially those which the Charter of that organization establishes, it is awaiting—in conformity with the information from Your Excellency in the telegram I am answering—that the United Command may enter into direct consultation with the Argentine Government.

The fact that this correspondence had a normal diffusion to the press aroused great disturbance and manifestations in the streets of the capital and at Rosario agitated against the intervention of Argentina in the hostilities. Although the Radical opposition was adverse to cooperation with the United States, the incidents in Rosario were stirred up by the Peronists themselves. Certain labor unions—the most important being *La Fraternidad*—authorized strikes in protest. The government hastened to deny the possibility of Argentine collaboration in arms. The chief of police accused extremist elements of spreading false rumors to the effect that the "government has already called up certain classes of the reserve" and that "Argentine troops are being enlisted for the fight in Korea."

That same night the foreign minister confirmed to the press that the answer of our country to the secretary general of the United Nations did not imply the sending of troops to the battle front. He maintained that such a measure in the internal sphere, from the point of view of the Constitution, would require the ratification of Congress. He insisted in fact that the reply to Trigve Lie did not exceed the limits of a mere acknowledgment of receiving a circular. Argentine collaboration was reduced to a simple shipment of food supplies.

Ratification of the Rio Treaty

The surprising ratification of the Rio Treaty by the Congress shortly after the first incidents in Korea had antecedents of a more pacific nature. The economic team that had replaced Miranda sought to improve relations with the United States and made serious efforts to amortize the Argentine debts in that country.

In February 1950, Assistant Secretary of State Edward G. Miller had arrived in Buenos Aires, and as a consequence of his visit the problems pending with various enterprises—Swift International, Braniff, Panagra, and Pan American—were liquidated in March and April. Shortly afterward, it was also possible to resolve the differences existing within the petroleum and the movie industries of the United States. Meanwhile, in search of more satisfactory results, representatives of both nations discussed

the possibilities of a new treaty and further agreements on investments and double taxation. Finally, in May, Minister of Finance
Cereijo traveled to the United States and held discussions with
various official personalities and private parties. On May 17, the
Export-Import Bank announced the approval of a credit of 125
million dollars to a group of Argentine banks under guarantee
of the Central Bank. The operation was designed exclusively to
wipe out the commercial debts of Argentine banks with their
North American correspondents.

Nevertheless, this liberality was not exempt from political
quid pro quo. In fact, two weeks before the announcement of
the credit, the May 4 edition of the New York Times reported
that the condition sine qua non for the Argentine-North American economic arrangement meant our country's ratification of
the military pacts of Rio de Janeiro.

The disturbance aroused by the first notices of the Korean
crisis offered the adequate framework for the rapid ratification of
a treaty that lay dormant for more than two years in the respective parliamentary commission. The Peronist majority in the
Chamber of Deputies tried to justify the sly form in which the
debate was planted, almost without previous notice, and the
bulk of the Radical opposition fought tenaciously against the
approval of the treaty. In the name of the latter, Frondizi
attacked the procedure that was followed in ratifying the treaty
and pointed out its probable causes:

> Immediate necessities of maintaining an economic stability,
> which [the government] did not know how to defend with
> a policy of effective undertakings, will today carry the nation
> to the Rio pact and perhaps tomorrow to the delivery of the
> petroleum and to the control of our economy.

The Washington Conference

On November 5, 1950, Communist China intervened openly

in the Korean War. With this the risk arose that this limited conflict would become a general one. For the purpose of confronting the new situation, the Fourth Meeting of Consultation of the American Foreign Ministers was convoked in Washington for March 1951, by which date the dangers had diminished.

The Argentine delegation was made up of Foreign Minister Paz, Jerónimo Remorino, Eusebio Campos, Oscar L. Pelliza, José Aloatti, José C. Vittone, Rodolfo Muñoz, and César A. Bunge.

In January the Perón government had seized the newspaper *La Prensa* in order to turn it over to the CGT (*Confederación General de Trabajo*). The echoes provoked by this shock had scarcely quieted when on the eve of the fourth consultation meeting, March 24, Perón revealed that thermonuclear reactions were being carried out on a technical scale under conditions of control, in the "pilot plant of atomic energy on the Island of Huemul of San Carlos de Bariloche."

With these contradictory signs, the Argentine delegation had to move in a conference whose program covered three themes: hemispheric defense (the United States wanted greater military cooperation from her neighbors); internal security (the United States was also seeking to improve control over communism); and economic advantages (suggested, of course, by Latin America).

The military project presented by the United States, Brazil, Colombia, El Salvador, Paraguay, and Uruguay in its dispositive part required the Inter-American Defense Board to propose to the governments, with some anticipation, its plans for the preparation of the armed forces and the defense of the hemisphere. Already in the respective commission, Argentina, Mexico, and Guatemala were opposing the intentions of turning over military contingents to an international organization.

In his speech Foreign Minister Paz cited constitutional norms as the reason for not invading the jurisdiction of Congress in military affairs. In spite of these legalistic scruples, Argentina voted for Resolution II, which recommended the contribution of efforts to the United Nations through collective security and the preparation of the armed forces elements for continental defense, in keeping with constitutional principles. Argentina, however, introduced an important reservation:

> In voting affirmatively in accordance with instructions from my government, and in spite of the provision in the text as to the resolution of the constitutional norms clause, I must formulate a reservation in the sense that every use of armed forces, whether in the world order or in the continental, is dependent upon the national Constitution, which reserves said power with its exclusive and nondelegable character to the Congress of the nation. And, furthermore, in this solemn opportunity, I wish to make expressly clear that my Government will not take any decision without the express consultation and decision of the Argentine people, because it is a question of the exercise appropriate to sovereignty and of a nontransferable attribute of the people.

ECONOMIC UNION

Meanwhile, reconciliation with the United States was not advancing, and Perón undertook the ambitious enterprise of achieving South American economic union. Although this initiative was not original—since in 1941, in the regional conference of the River Plate countries, the formation of a customs union had been proposed—Perón gave it a strong but ephemeral impulse. The motives were diverse: yearnings for leadership, obtaining markets for exportable surplus, and greater support for opposing the United States. The effort was developed throughout 1953, only to collapse prior to the rapprochement with Washington.

In February of that year Perón visited Chile, and on February 21, in the Salón Rojo of the Moneda, he signed an agreement destined to favor economic unity between both countries, which was called the "Act of Santiago," a forerunner of the treaty which was to be signed in Buenos Aires six months later. The latter enumerated a series of general principles on economic complementarism; lowering of customs duties and freedom from taxation; coordination of exchange; reciprocal interchange of the principal national products; and credit facilities. It created a common central organ, the General Council of the Chilean-Argentine Economic Union, in order to promote plans and projects that would carry into practice the ends sought.

On returning from his Chilean trip, which aroused jealousy in Brazil, Perón published a decalogue which fixed the duties of Argentines with respect to the Trans-Andean nation. Without forgetting the sovereignty of the Chilean nation, the Argentines must regard the Chileans as compatriots. The fourth article of the decalogue states: "The Government, the State and the Argentine people will assemble all their resources to consolidate in Chile social justice, political sovereignty, and economic independence."

On August 13 Perón traveled to Asunción in order to return to Paraguay the trophies of the War of 1865 and to sign an agreement of economic union—as the first step toward a customs union. In this way Paraguay became the first country of the continent to adhere to the invitation formulated in the Act of Santiago. The characteristics of the treaty were similar to those of the antecedent, and again the corresponding decalogue was not lacking. As with the Chilean pact, a mixed council was formed of representatives from each one of the signatories.

The exotic note in this program of continental economic union was provided by the dictator of Nicaragua, Anastasio Samoza, who on the occasion of his visit to Argentina adhered to the new union by means of the so-called Declaration of Buenos Aires, signed October 17, 1953. (Under the Perón regime October 17 was celebrated as "Loyalty Day.")

On December 12 the foreign ministers of Ecuador and Argentina signed in Quito an act of economic union between both countries. This instrument declared its express adherence to the Act of Santiago. The solidarity with Bolivia was made known early in September 1954, while Brazil, Peru, and Uruguay, in spite of receiving invitations, refused to incorporate themselves into the treaty.

As noted above, the improvement of Argentine relations with the Republican administration of General Eisenhower tended to lessen the importance of these efforts, for the Peronist energies were now oriented toward the former adversary.

THE SHADOW OF ARBENZ

In 1954 the internal situation of Guatemala gave concern because of the danger that it could become a communist bridgehead in America. The United States, fearing that the hemispheric security was being threatened, proposed the Tenth Inter-American Conference, which took place in Caracas from March 1 to 28. The Argentine delegation was composed of Foreign Minister Remorino, José C. Vittone, Rodolfo Muñoz, Julio de Tezanos Pinto, Julio Abal, Oscar E. Pelliza, Luis Camps, and César A. Bunge.

Although the program of the Conference also contained economic, social, and cultural matters, the issue that aroused greater interest was the political one, especially the intervention of international communism in the American republics. To obtain a resolution against communism was the principal purpose of the United States delegation. On their part, the Latin American nations placed more emphasis on economic problems. As in all the earlier conferences, they sought to obtain greater economic cooperation as well as a solution for the drop in prices of raw materials as compared with manufactured products. Shortly after arrival in Caracas, Remorino advanced the causal nexus between both problems.

The low prices for raw materials imply and oblige low wages, which are incitations for the working class that often lead it to the edge of misery, and it is precisely here that the people develop exotic ideas. In this very way there is a direct relation between this economic problem of low wages and the social situations of America, which would be very important to approach.

Foster Dulles, who headed the North American delegation, presented a project for resolution destined to eliminate communism from the hemisphere. Argentina, through Rodolfo Muñoz —Remorino had already left the Conference—insisted that the problem dividing the world ideologically ought to find solutions in the improvement of the conditions of life. The communist threat, in his judgment, would not change the dogma of self-determination:

In view of the proposals presented up to now, we believe that the decision which this conference adopts ought to contain a clause that expressly recognizes the right of the peoples to choose their own systems of government. Any ambiguity in this respect might permit the conclusion that under the pretext of protecting them from some future event, we are giving a death blow to the free determination of the peoples of America.

Later on the Argentine delegation tried to avoid application of the condemnation of communism to Guatemala, and Muñoz criticized the fact that this Conference would refer to this concrete case. "Placing ourselves in a position free of euphemisms, we have heard with pleasure that the proposals under discussion are not directed against any state, but we understand at the same time the attitude of a sister republic that feels herself affected."

He concluded with the request that the drafting of the original proposal be modified so as not allude to international communism, but to all extracontinental aggression, in order that the declaration may be a matter of international policy and not of internal policy.

On March 13, there was approval of Resolution XCIII, called the "Declaration of Solidarity for the Preservation of Political Integrity of the American States Against the Intervention of International Communism," which disposed:

> That the domination or control of the political institutions of any American State by the international Communist movement, extending to this hemisphere the political system of an extra-continental power, would constitute a threat to the sovereignty and political independence of the American States, endangering the peace of America, and would call for a meeting of consultation to consider the adoption of measures in accordance with existing treaties.

The importance of this resolution—approved with the abstention of Argentina and Mexico, and voted against by Guatemala —lies in the fact that it designates the establishment of communism in any American state as a premise for the application of the Rio Treaty.

In connection with the economic proposals, the Latin American delegations obtained no practical advantages other than mere declarations. Nor did our country win from the United States support for a proposal on the disposal of the agricultural surplus. However, as H. F. Peterson notes, nothing of what happened in Caracas succeeded in disturbing the recent calm in the relations between the United States and Argentina.

PERÓN AND HIS OPPONENTS

A strong electoral support along with his Latin American prestige gave Perón the basis for his initial position regarding the United States. To this must be added the erroneous belief that the then favorable position of Argentina in the world markets would be maintained without change throughout the postwar period, or that it would even improve in the case of a third conflagration breaking out—a possibility he regarded as certain.

Ideological and psychological motivations do not alone explain his anti-Yankee attitude after the fall of Braden. In the economic field, it will be recalled, Perón tried an anachronistic statist autarky that violently opposed North American efforts in elimication of the Rio Treaty and the loan obtained from the Export the United States on the level of world strategy, but also sought to discover a new road between capitalism and socialism.

United States. In 1951 the first step was evident with the ratifinating barriers to international trade. For the "third position" not only signified a Utopian equidistance between Russia and But the breakdown of his economic policy forced Perón to abandon opportunistic neutralism and to draw nearer to the Import Bank. Moreover, early in the Republican administration, the visit of Milton Eisenhower (July 1953) accelerated a rapprochement, which before had only been insinuated. The Argentine Congress passed an investment law establishing guarantees for foreign contributions. Under its protection Henry Kaiser's investments were soon established in the country, and negotiations were undertaken with the Atlas Corporation. Finally, Perón, convinced of the insufficiency of YPF (*Yacimientos Petrolíferas Fiscales*), in order to achieve petroleum self-sufficiency, signed a contract with a subsidiary enterprise of the Standard Oil of California and was in advanced negotiations with the Royal Dutch Shell and the Standard Oil of New Jersey. Also, by the time of his downfall he was negotiating a loan with the Export Import Bank for a value of 60 million dollars to install a steel plant.

While Perón was gradually drawing nearer to the United States, the opposition, by a curious phenomenon of political polarization, was moving in the opposite direction. The components of the *Unión Democrática* had based their electoral campaign of 1946 on the triumph of the Allies and the accusation of Nazism leveled against Perón. Only the disciples of Moisés Lebensohn, who formed the left wing of the *Unión Cívica Radical*, took for themselves in this moment the banners of anti-imperialism and sought to surpass Perón himself in this field. Intellectually gifted, they headed the parliamentary opposition to Peronism and would not limit themselves to coinciding on certain points of the official foreign policy, for example, with respect to the Havana Conference of 1947–1948.

In August, 1949, Frondizi remarked in the Chamber of Deputies: "Tonight I have already said that I was in agreement with the Argentine attitude in refusing to sign these protocols. I now ratify that I have no fear of coinciding in principles in which one ought to coincide on behalf of the general interest." These deputies went even farther, because they reached the point of suggesting concrete attitudes such as the rejection of the Bretton Woods Pacts, a suggestion welcomed and accepted by the government.

Later this group severely criticized Perón's attempts to draw nearer to the United States, made an active campaign against the ratification of the Rio Treaty (June 1950), kept a significant silence during the communist aggression in Korea and did not hide sympathies for Arévalo and Arbenz in the Guatemala case.

But the Radical intransigents, in their desire to surpass Perón, not only dragged along the rest of the opposition to a neutralist and anti-Yankee attitude but also tried to surpass his statist and interventionist concepts of the economy. Little by little, for the same reasons whereby they replaced sympathy for the Allies with distrust of the United States, they were adopting a position adverse to the capitalist system and to private initiative in order to subscribe to a socializing ideology. Thus when Perón reached an understanding with North American businessmen, the opposition made of the contract with the California Standard Oil one of its principal points. And Frondizi, in his radio speech during the short period of the Peronist "pacification" in 1955, almost equated the Argentine crisis to this problem.

From the time of Braden and the *Unión Democrática*, Perón as well as his opposition had run a long road full of surprises.

7: BETWEEN EAST AND WEST

THE LIBERATING REVOLUTION

In foreign affairs the Revolution that deposed Perón took the measures necessary to withdraw the country from the isolation in which the "third position" had left it. Up to this point Argentina had not ratified even essential instruments, either in the hemispheric order or in the world order.

By Decree-Law 328 of January 14, 1956, the Revolutionary government ratified the charter of the OAS. One of the clauses stated:

> That it is the purpose of the Provisional government to favor the strengthening of the fraternal links uniting the Argentine people with the sister nations of America.

Thus was perfected juridically an act begun eight years earlier in the Ninth Inter-American Conference of Bogotá. Ours was the last country of the hemisphere to regularize its situation with respect to the OAS.

The ratification of the Bretton-Woods Agreement—sent by the Perón government to the Congress, but later withdrawn on the initiative of the Radical opposition—was carried out early by means of Decree-Law 15,970, also in 1956. In this way, the country entered the International Monetary Fund and the International Bank for Reconstruction and Development.

The Act of Paris

In 1947 the first steps toward the multilateralization of trade in Western Europe had been taken. The Organization for European Economic Cooperation (OEEC), then set up, imposed on its members the obligation of liberalizing exchange between the countries of Western Europe, in that the European Payments Union (EPU) created in 1950 also formalized a regime of multilateral payments with monthly liquidation of balances. Argentina had preferred, up to 1955, a "strict bilateralism." But in 1956 the Revolutionary government decided to undertake discussions and reorganize its international commerce on multilateral bases. This Argentine initiative brought with it consultations with the European countries. At one of these consultations, carried out in the headquarters of the OEEC, the Argentine government was invited to name an observer. Roberto Verrier, then undersecretary of finance, fulfilled this role at the Paris meeting; after various negotiations in several European capitals, he agreed with the representatives of the eleven European countries participating in the common discussions on the bases for the multilateral regime of trade and payments.

The instrument, called the "Act of Paris," stated the general principles of multilateral regime and of the consolidation within ten years of the official and commercial debts of Argentina, both short and medium term. Both aspects of the act—the multilateral regime of trade and payments, as well as the consolidation of the debts—were closely linked between themselves, and they combined, toward the same end, the reimbursement of the debt at moderate interest. In London, June 1956, there was a meeting of experts from central banks, attended by Argentine delegates. In this meeting they agreed upon technical norms for placing in action the regulations effective as of July 2, 1956.

During the talks that brought about the Act of Paris, it was foreseen that Argentina would undertake negotiations with each one of the participating countries. On July 2 Argentina implemented the multilateral system with nine countries: Austria, Belgium, Switzerland, United Kingdom, France, Denmark,

Sweden, and Norway. Italy adhered on August 3, 1956, but the Federal Republic of Germany participated in the multilateral system only after November 25, 1957. In this way Germany entered the definitive system without having been part of the transitory multilateral regime.

After more than twenty-three years of application the bilateral system, begun with the signing of the Roca-Runciman Agreement, was finally put aside and the country entered fully into multilateralism.

A HAPPY BEGINNING

The official acts of the first months of the presidency of Frondizi followed the international line traced by the Liberating Revolution. Only an excessively suspicious eye could have discerned in the speeches given by the President-Elect throughout Latin America (April, 1958) the two germs that would later result in irreparable errors—one being the inordinate commendation of the Brazilian situation:

> The Argentine people admire Brazil for her national conscience, the clear prestige of her institutions, the high standards of culture. . . . For all that I have been able to confirm, and I repeat it with profound sincerity, as Americans we are proud of Brazil.
>
> We Argentines have much in common with Brazil: race, history, and religion; her institutions inspire in us identical ideals of national realization, social progress, and respect for the human being. We feel as if these are our efforts that Brazil is carrying out in order to achieve the materialization of such aspirations. Every triumph of Brazil in the field of technology, science, or culture is a triumph of ours, an American triumph.

Perhaps the hyperbole can be attributed simply to the norms of international courtesy and not to authentic admiration for a country of such widely acknowledged contrasts.

The other point is the dissolution of the Western idea, which seems obvious in these speeches of the President-Elect, and which later is reproduced in the paragraphs dedicated to foreign policy in his first message to Congress May 1, 1958. Argentina belongs to the West, but this concept does not signify for Frondizi an option, a resignation of universality. For him the West "is not a condition of antagonism." A similar neutralized version of the Argentine position in the world was to reappear frequently in the international texts of the Frondizi government.

Meanwhile a change full of consequences was slowly taking place on the Latin American horizon. The movement against the Batista regime in Cuba triumphed, and on January 3, 1959, the rebel troops burst into Havana to offer a short interregnum of liberty on this Caribbean Island.

A few days later Frondizi became the first Argentine president to visit the United States. In addressing himself to the North American Congress, he planted his notion of the underdevelopment of Latin America, not failing to add:

> To leave in stagnation an American country is as dangerous as an attack that could come from an extracontinental power. Fighting the backwardness of peoples calls for a greater solidarity within the hemisphere than that occasioned by its political or military defense. The true defense of the continent consists in eliminating the causes that give rise to the misery and injustice in cultural retardation.

This phrase appeared theoretical in the moments when the euphoria of the Cuban liberation was flooding all of America. Later events rendered it partially prophetic—if not with regard to the policy prescribed by the visitor, at least with respect to the future attitude that he and his administration would seek to inspire in Argentina.

But other expressions of Frondizi were without doubt more apt to comfort his hosts, such as that wherein he rejected the supposition of an eventual invitation from him to Mikoyan to visit Argentina, because "these visits of persons of ideology alien to our manner of being are not of interest to us."

In May 1959, on the occasion of the Committee of the Twenty-One meeting in Buenos Aires, Fidel Castro headed the Cuban delegation. It was here that he formulated his politics of extortion with the United States, a system whereby he immediately obtained quick followers in the hemisphere. Textually he said:

> The technicians of the Cuban delegation have calculated that economic development of Latin America, if a full development of Latin America is to be truly achieved, needs a financing of 30 billion dollars in a period of ten years.
> . . . I declare that our needs can be met only through the United States and through public financing . . . and this is the procedure the United States has employed in Europe and in the Near East. Why then should Latin America disregard this opportunity, one that was deemed best for the others?

The Senate, in August 1959, refused consent for the designation of the former Foreign Minister Florit as ambassador to the OAS. Three months earlier, it had taken the same course with regard to the nominations of Dardo Cúneo and Alfredo Allende because they belonged, as it was brought out, to the Frigerio line.

During the latter part of August—on the initiative of Brazil, Chile, the United States, and Peru—the Fifth Meeting of the Foreign Ministers convened in Santiago de Chile for the purpose of preserving peace in the Caribbean Zone and of strengthening the principle of nonintervention and protection of human rights. The Argentine delegation included Foreign Minister Taboada and Ambassadors Luis M. de Pablo Pardo and Luis S. Sanz, as well as Raúl Rodríguez Araya, Oscar H. Camilión, Jorge Gardella, Enrique Ross, Ernesto de la Guardia, Vicente Berasategui, and Julio Barbosa.

For the first time, the machinery of consultation was brought into action by purely American causes and not as a consequence of world events, as had happened in the four previous meetings. The concrete motives were the invasions by groups of armed Castroites in Panama, Nicaragua, and the Dominican Republic (between April and July 1959). In turn, the latter country had leveled a similar action against Cuba.

Nevertheless, under the impression of the Dominican reprisal, the Cuban delegation, with support from Venezuela, introduced another point in the conference: the exclusion of dictatorial governments from OAS and the censure for the violation of human rights on the part of the Dominican government in repressing the invasion of its territory by elements proceeding from Cuba a month earlier. This idea, which by an irony of history would be used against Cuba herself at Punta del Este in January 1962, was then defended by Foreign Minister Raúl Roa, who even reached the point of saying that international force applied to governments to make them respect human rights is not intervention (*La Prensa*, August 4, 1959).

The Fifth Meeting of Consultation approved unanimously the "Declaration of Santiago," whose content incorporated into the inter-American system principles that impinged on the domestic order, such as the independence of the judicial power, the necessity for free elections, the guarantee of the fundamental rights of the human person and the freedom of expression in all its forms. It also condemned perpetuation in power and the systematic use of political proscription.

Foreign Minister Taboada, in speaking at the United Nations Assembly in September 1959, emphasized the Argentine position as contrary to all neutralism:

It is appropriate to leave perfectly clear that this moderating mission of the medium and small powers does not necessarily imply equidistance with regard to the ideological positions in dispute. In what concerns Argentina, we here ratify once more complete solidarity with the line of the West, to which she belongs by origin, by spiritual affinity and by geographical position.

Between June 14 and July 10, 1960, Frondizi, in accordance with his farewell message to the Argentine people, visited nine countries of Western Europe in pursuit of two fundamental objectives: to strengthen relations with the friendly European nations and to forestall the restrictive tendencies against Latin America that were being insinuated in the Old Continent by means of new economic regional organizations. To these ends must be added that of winning European support for the plan of stabilization and development. In all his talks throughout Europe, Frondizi guarded against repeating his views on the dissolution of the Western idea, outlined above. On the contrary, he referred on more than one occasion to the "Western Bloc," in the strict sense, in order to require aid from its rich members for the benefit of Latin America, the "only deficiently developed zone of the West." This last concept, reiterated in all the stages of his European trip, was perhaps his main drive. Before leaving for Europe, the President had already indicated: "We are convinced that the present system, geared toward a sense of the West, can be guaranteed only with the intelligent and equitable articulation of a policy of international economic cooperation."

In such a text it was logical to insert the exhortation directed by the Argentine government to the Cubans urging the renunciation of links that were twisting the original direction of the uprising against Batista. The Soviet Union had announced (July 9, 1960), via all means of publicity within reach, its military support—including the threat of intercontinental bombardment —for the Castro regime, which in turn was piling up proofs of a decided inclination toward the communist world. On July 13 our Foreign Ministry sent the following telegram to the Argentine Embassy at Havana:

I beg Your Excellency to transmit urgently to the Cuban authorities in the name of the Argentine government that it is seriously concerned with the international consequences that might arise from threats formulated by an extrahemispheric state, shaping up as intervention in hemispheric affairs. The Argentine government requests the government of Cuba to express its disapproval of all manifestations that signify meddling of extrahemispheric powers in American affairs.

THE CHANGE OF DIRECTION

The just motives of concern, which the Argentine government felt in the face of the Cuban deviation, soon alarmed the rest of the continent. Therefore, the American foreign ministers at San José, Costa Rica, treated not only the problem planted by the Dominican Republic, but also the extracontinental threats and subversive activities. Thus the Dominican case became the purpose of the Sixth Meeting of Consultation; and immediately after, the Seventh Meeting was devoted to communist meddling in the politics of the hemisphere.

The Argentine delegation at both meetings was headed by Foreign Minister Taboada and comprised of Luis M. de Pablo Pardo, Arnoldo T. Musich, Ezequiel V. Pereyra, Raúl A. Medina Muñoz, Enrique J. Ross, Vicente B. Berasategui, Ramón A. Salem, Mario A. Cámpora, and the National Deputy Juan C. Manes. Also present at San José were the Argentine ambassadors to the OAS and Costa Rica, Emilio D. del Carril and Luis E. Vera. Later on our ambassador at Havana, Julio C. Amoedo, was called on for consultation.

The "Double Instructions"

The instructions that were to be binding on the delegation were elaborated through the normal channels of the Foreign

Ministry and approved by Frondizi. They pointed out the adherence of our country to the West, as well as the "activity of forces alien to the inter-American community" having objectives "incompatible with the institutional style of democratic deep-rootedness" of the continent. Accordingly, these instructions authorized the delegation to intervene "actively in the negotiations and the decisions which have as their objective the preservation of democratic institutions against the activity of international communism." Above all, it was provided in the document that:

> The manifestations made by an extracontinental power, which imply virtually the threat of a foreign state to intervene in continental affairs, ought to receive from the meeting of consultation a clear and definite reply that reaffirms the solidarity of the American states in the face of the threat of intervention and, at the same time, the rejection of the threat because it endangers peace.

And this situation was to be met by the resources provided by the inter-American system.

The third paragraph of the instructions contained a discreet allusion to the problem of cooperation for economic development and the convenience of harmonious links between the activities in the inter-American sphere and the economic groupings of the Western world.

When the principal Argentine delegates were already enroute by air to San José, Minister Musich informed them of the "new instructions" from Frondizi. Immediately there was discord concerning the text to be followed by the delegation—a struggle that lasted throughout the entire trip and during the two meetings in Costa Rica. Ambassador de Pablo Pardo defended the original instructions, and Minister Musich those which he had carried while Foreign Minister Taboada oscillated between the two positions.

When our mission made a brief stop at Panama, the original instructions received support from Commander in Chief of the Army General Carlos S. Toranzo Montero, who by coincidence was in the Canal Zone to attend a meeting connected with hemispheric defense. Shortly after the beginning of the Sixth Meeting of Consultation, Taboada and certain members of the delegation held a conference with Secretary of State Christian Herter and other North American officials. The agenda of the Sixth Meeting—convoked on the initiative of Venezuela, by reason of the occurrences of the Dominican Republic—demonstrated agreement between the delegations of both Argentina and the United States.

Disagreement, however, arose by way of the economic points singled out with greater emphasis in the "second instructions" from the Argentine government. Herter recalled President Eisenhower's plan of aid, which had recently been approved by the Senate, and insisted with firmness that the United States did not want to see itself dragged by force to this cooperation. The North American aid would be free and spontaneous and should not be mixed up with the political proposals in these consultation meetings.

Foreign Minister Taboada cabled Buenos Aires a synthesis of his conversations with the secretary of state, and on August 19 Undersecretary Centeno replied that Argentina would not seek to use pressure or to confuse the economic collaboration with the case of Cuba. But he did not fail to add that it would be convenient to bring up "if it should be opportune" the problem of highways and airports as well as that of the consequences of unemployment—themes that previously had been presented by Frondizi to Eisenhower, to Thomas Mann, and to Chargé d'Affaires Bernbaum in Buenos Aires. The North American position was ratified by Mann to Musich, and in connection with this interview Taboada directed to Frondizi a new dispatch (August 20), estimating that for the United States the economic proposal would be "considered aggressive and contrary to the object" of the Meeting of Consultation. Therefore, he requested that points 9 and 10 of the "second instructions" be confirmed or rectified. The immediate official reply was that of maintaining both points, adapting them to the development of the conference. On August 22 Musich telegraphed the Foreign Ministry that Taboada, del Carril, and he were in accord in presenting the proposal to implement points 9 and 10.

Meanwhile, the American foreign ministers had brought to an end the Sixth Meeting of Consultation with a resolution by virtue of which the following collective measures were provided: rupture of diplomatic relations with the Dominican Republic; partial interruptions of economic relations with the same country, beginning with the immediate suspension of traffic in arms and instruments of war. The council of the OAS would study the possibility of extending the suspension of trade to other articles in accordance with constitutional and legal dispositions of the member states. The council was authorized to suspend by two-thirds majority the application of the measures to the Dominican Republic when it ceased to "constitute a source of danger for the peace and security of the hemisphere."

Immediately, the Seventh Meeting of Consultation began. Its primordial end was to confront the extracontinental threat in America and the concrete acts of communist subversion. On August 22, 1960, the Argentine delegation presented a project relative to the struggle against communism and revolutionary war. The dispositive part provided for the convoking of a special conference within ninety days to elaborate and prepare a treaty on: (1) rights and obligations of the states participating in the struggle against communism; (2) the most suitable methods to combat communism without excluding the founding, if it should be convenient, of a specialized inter-American organism. In addition, it would be required of the Inter-American Defense Board to provide a technical report on revolutionary war, as well as the means of preventing it and repressing it, "within the framework of the common defense of the hemisphere." The cable, in which Taboada reported to the Argentine government the presentation of the project, received a surprising reply from Buenos Aires, signed by Undersecretary Centeno and directed exclusively to the foreign minister:

> The President expresses that he received knowledge of the Argentine presentation through newspaper report. He asks to be consulted directly before adopting decisions not previously agreed upon.

Did the proposal against communism annoy Frondizi? Actually Taboada did not delay in answering him that the initiative resulted from the instructions received, and that he was unaware of any press commentaries because he had not made any declaration to the press. At this point, the foreign minister was very close to resigning his post right in the middle of the conference.

A cable from Musich to Centeno on August 24 emphasized North American concern over the Argentine attitude: "If the government should vary the position assumed during the last two years, it would prejudice the political stability of the continent." Washington was regarding Argentina as an essential factor in this stability and would therefore try to strengthen the weak points in the Argentine economic program.

Finally, the Seventh Meeting of Consultation unanimously approved—in the absence of the Dominican Republic and Cuba —a resolution by which the intervention or threat of intervention from outside the hemisphere in America was condemned, along with "the pretension of the Sino-Soviet powers to utilize the political, economic, or social situation of any American State with the purpose of destroying the continental unity and of placing in danger the peace and security of the hemisphere."

There was also reaffirmation of the principle of nonintervention; the incompatibility of the inter-American system with all forms of totalitarianism; and the obligation of all states to submit themselves to the discipline of the voluntarily and freely agreed upon system. The resolution concluded with an exhortation for the pacific settlement of bilateral disputes and with a vote of confidence in the OAS.

The colophon of Costa Rica was in the form of insulting declarations, which the Cuban Foreign Minister Roa on his return to Havana let loose against several Latin American chiefs of state. He described Frondizi as the "viscous concretion of the worst human excrescences." Apart from a *pro forma* protest from the Foreign Ministry, this colorful definition did not dissuade the Argentine government from its design to protect Cuba.

The following month the third meeting of the Committee of the Twenty-One took place in Bogotá. Musich headed the Argentine delegation, among whose members were Dardo Cúneo and Horacio Rodríguez Larreta. The United States offered 500 million dollars to Latin America; however, the proposal aroused the criticism of Brazil and Argentina, because it did not include long-term loans payable in local currency for certain plans of development, such as roads, communications, and hydroelectric centers. On September 7 Musich said in his speech:

> The Committee of the Twenty-One must fill an economic vacuum left by the conference of foreign ministers in Costa Rica. We believe it necessary that America resolve to attack the unjust situation of underdevelopment in which she finds herself, and in this sense we support Operation Pan-America by trying to adopt it and transform it into an effective action with all the international imagination that was applied to the reconstruction of Europe.

Or, it could have been that the Bogotá meeting, in the eyes of the Argentine representative, was the revenge for the Meetings of Consultation of Costa Rica. He added:

What, very much to our regret, was not faced then with resolute decision, must be treated here and now. The possibility of doing it favors us, as we are freed of all ideological meddling. There is only one way to attack from the front the political instability in various sectors of the continent.

For his proposals he would require a new organization, politically autonomous, economic in character, which would receive its political orientation from an annual meeting of technicians. It is obvious that such a proposal sought to offset the OAS. In order to carry it out, it would be necessary to convoke a special conference and to reform the charter of that organization.

The Politics of Extortion

In the attitude of the government and in that of the Argentine delegation to Costa Rica, the technique of soliciting economic advantages from the United States in exchange for urgent political measures already stood out with complete clarity. This extortionist procedure was initiated crudely by Fidel Castro himself during his visit to Buenos Aires in May 1959, when he required of Washington the sum of 30 billion dollars for Latin America.

Frondizi's top staff quickly took over this system and not only exercised it in practice but even dared to undertake its theoretical formulation, the justification of the scheme as the "foreign policy in the service of development." It is not a prejudice to maintain that such a focus in foreign relations suffers from historical materialism, because the concrete cases confirm this ideological deviation, and none more clearly than Cuba.

Nobody then doubted that in the suffering Caribbean island the democratic revolution against Batista had been gradually captured by means of an extended *golpe de estado*, which of course the revolutionary circumstances themselves and their inevitable regime of exception were favoring. This vision of the Cuban drama was not discussed until the staff assistants of President Frondizi discovered that Cuba had been a victim of economic underdevelopment and not of international communism. However improbable this interpretation might be, it continued to be useful in upholding the myth of Argentine development set forth by the government, both within the country and especially abroad in the United States. Cuba then became not a hemispheric danger, but a living and permanent parable for the North Americans—an example of what might happen in the rest of Latin America if the United States were not generous in her aid—much like the sores of the professional beggars that ever keep open and never are cured, lest the alms cease.

The United States must choose between the Argentine "development" and the Cuban communist revolution, or better said with the title of a work by Frigerio, originator of this policy— "*Cuba o Argentina. Dos alternativas para un problema común: el subdesarrollo*" (March, 1961). Frigerio's thesis can be synthesized in one of his paragraphs:

> If the great industrial powers of the West do not act with rapidity and decision in this sense, the underdeveloped world will accept the aid of the other sector. No ideological consideration is capable of preventing it, because for these countries nothing is more important than their national interests in progress. It is important to be realistic in this and not to let oneself be deceived by proposals contrary to the irreversible direction of history. Cuba is demonstrating this in our hemisphere. Suffocated by an agrarian economy of quasi monoculture, it has this dilemma: to diversify its production and industrialize, or to perish.

This thesis of Frigerio's was recited almost literally by Frondizi to President Kennedy on September 26, 1961. The following is part of his own report of the interview released to the Argentine people thirteen days later:

> Cuba and Argentina are the two opposing countries in the

foreseeable process of Latin America. Argentina exemplifies a behavior which can be exhibited with pride before all America. It is proceeding to the rapid transformation of its economic structure. The path of Cuba is that of subversion, that of destruction, of values which Latin America has created with bloody and exhausting sacrifices. Argentina's path is that of preservation of these values, that of a progress within freedom and respect for the dignity of the human being.

Cuba was not a threat for the peace and security of the hemisphere, as certain states even geographically remote from the island were finding out in their own flesh but a point of reference, a term of indispensable comparison with the triumphal Argentine "development."

In books and articles writers of the Frigerio school insisted on this singular focus of the problem. The young former Foreign Minister Florit, after recalling with erudition that Hegel excluded America from history and condemned it to prehistory, added some significant words:

> In our Latin American case it is important to point out that an episode in this process [of prehistory] is what has made us enter into world history. Better said, to obtain on part of the others the recognition of our condition as the countries that now stand within history. Unfortunately, this case is called Cuba and, also unfortunately, our entrance into world history has been made by the entrance route into our hemisphere of an episode of the so-called cold war.

The Cuban situation permitted Argentina to increase its bargaining power with the United States. Therefore, our attitude regarding the Cuban case had to be prudent and wary. We must avoid an ideological Westernism—disinterested and therefore economically without gain.

Frondizi's singular diplomacy was explained in March 1961 by Undersecretary of Foreign Relations Oscar H. Camilión, in the army's *Centro de Altos Estudios:*

. . . Argentina is a Latin American country, that is to say, she is made up of a geographical area belonging to the under-developed continents of the world, but she has conditions of negotiations that are very inferior to those of the other areas by virtue of her lesser strategic significance. Latin America, as a region remote from the immediate zones of conflict, has available much less "bargaining power" than the Afro-Asian countries. Also the region does not include any uncommitted countries and, in consequence, it has been accorded a relegated position in the order of priorities of the great powers of the West in their programs of economic cooperation. Our present solidarity with Latin America rises not only from the obvious traditional sympathy by reason of blood and language, but also from the conscience that only action can call attention to our necessities, as was demonstrated, though in limited measure, by the partial success achieved with Operation Pan-America.

From the new nations of Asia and Africa, Argentina would also learn new methods to turn herself into a great world power.

The Frustrated "Arbiter"

As the opposite pole of Argentine "development," Cuba henceforth would be carefully protected by the diplomacy of Frondizi so as not to fail to provoke, by contrast, its beneficial effects on our country.

One must not discount the influence exercised on the Argentine diplomatic direction by the victory of Alfredo L. Palacios as senator for the Federal District in the elections of February 5, 1961. Palacios obtained 315,646 votes against 309,194 for the opposing candidate of the People's Radical Party. The narrow difference of scarcely more than 6,000 votes, as well as the personal characteristics of the victor, did not prevent many observers from attributing the victory to the openly pro-Castro cam-

paign with which the Argentine Socialist Party had carried
Palacios into the Senate.

On February 17, our foreign minister rejected an Ecuadorian
proposal to begin a joint action of conciliatory character on the
part of the Latin American states in order to resolve the differences between Cuba and the United States. The Argentine negative resulted from the fact that many Latin American countries
were also in conflict with Cuba, and that it would be better to
wait until these interested parties were in a better position to
consider the offer, because to begin negotiations in this political
moment "could signify the wasting of an advantage to which it
would be difficult to return after a negative result." Nevertheless,
only sixteen days later—and having as a basis only a circular note
from the Cuban foreign minister, in which it was requested that
the countries which had not yet broken with Havana make use
of their good will in order to avoid the generalization of this rupture—the Argentine government suddenly interposed its good
offices in the conflict between Cuba and the United States.

By means of two telegrams, the Foreign Ministry reported its
initiative to both countries; it also announced to them that it
would designate two special ambassadors for the purpose of carrying out its initiative. These turned out to mean Miguel Ángel
Cárcano for Washington and Carlos M. Muñiz for Havana.

And from the first moment the Argentine offer received a
cold and distressful reception, not only from the United States,
but also from Cuba. The latter country was the first to respond
sourly:

> . . . the conduct of the Government of the United States of
> North America and the declarations and pronouncements of
> its officials made plain that that Government does not accept
> initiatives or any formula which might bring about bilateral
> discussion between both Governments of the existing differ-
> ences. Therefore, the Cuban Government believes that it is
> lamentably useless to initiate any action in this respect while

the Government of the United States of North America does not assume an attitude favorable to negotiation *through bilateral channels* on a plane of equality and with an open agenda of its differences with the Cuban Government, for which discussion we reiterate our favorable disposition.

The North American reply was longer in coming, and one of the paragraphs of Secretary of State Dean Rusk was not lacking in irony:

I venture also to express the belief that the Government of Your Excellency recognizes the reality of the capture of the Cuban revolution by the Sino-Soviet bloc, and that your preoccupation with respect to this process was the occasion of the telegram which Your Excellency sent me, on the date of March 4.*

And then, after alluding to the rupture of the Cuban links with the communist powers, and to its obligations under the inter-American system, Rusk's note concludes:

If the Government of the Argentine Republic could establish that the Government of Cuba is disposed to take effective steps to reach these ends, the Government of the United States, after this determination, would be delighted to be able to discuss with the Government of Your Excellency this *hemispheric* problem.*

In this picturesque episode one must see something more serious than the overwhelming Argentine failure: the support of our Foreign Ministry for the Cuban thesis of bilateral conflict with the United States. In the text of both notes the key words have been underscored. While Cuba sought to embody a bilateral difference with the United States, the latter country maintained that the Castro problem was hemispheric, that it was a matter of concern for all the American states. In offering its good offices

* Translated from Argentine press accounts.

that would soon be frustrated, the Argentine government was already admitting the Cuban focus of the problem.

Faced with internal discontent the government was lavish with explanations of its attitude, which were hardly very clear. Foreign Minister Taboada told the press on March 7: "Our undertaking was in accordance with the antecedent of the note from Dr. Roa, which although it did not ask for mediation, at least placed in disposition the offering of good offices"; and a declaration from the Foreign Ministry on March 13 insisted on the theme of development but omitted any explanation of why the proposal from Ecuador had been rejected days before the Argentine undertaking was effected. It is appropriate to point out that in this moment the government was beginning the practice of the unexpected gestures and confused explanations, above all, in the field of foreign policy.

The military context can throw some light in this respect. During this time the influence of General Carlos S. Toranzo Montero in the direction of the army was deteriorating rapidly. With his request for release on March 22, Frondizi and his staff felt themselves free of any military vigilance or pressure, and they undertook their boldest political adventures with results which are already known.

At the time of the interposition of our good offices with so little success, Frondizi was not in Buenos Aires, but on a trip south—culminating in a visit to the Antarctic on March 8, which aroused angry British and Chilean reactions. The first were somewhat ironic, the second rather bitter. In Buenos Aires a treaty had just been signed to put an end to the old questions of territorial limits with a neighboring nation. Ratification from the Chilean Congress was still required, but Frondizi's trip to the Antarctic led both the government supporters in the Senate and the opposition to postpone indefinitely the consideration of the protocol signed with Argentina. Our government made the problem somewhat worse by sending as ambassador to Santiago

Luis M. de Pablo Pardo, whom the Chilean nationalists regarded as the principal craftsman of the treaties with Argentina. This designation could be interpreted as a personal vengeance. The gratuitous conflict with Chile led Deputy Mathov to ask later in the Congress if the episode beginning with Frondizi's trip to the Antarctic was not perhaps a diversionary maneuver, alien to the national interests.

TRAILING BRAZIL

The apparent simplification of the military panorama coincided with the 1961 electoral victories of the government. The official party won in the elections at Catamarca on March 5, in Rosario March 19, in Misiones and San Luis April 9. Both these circumstances encouraged the government to undertake even more daring maneuvers in foreign policy.

Between April 20 and 22, Frondizi held a meeting with Janio Quadros, the new president of Brazil who had taken office three months before. The result of these discussions was the Treaty of Friendship and Consultation, signed in Uruguayana on April 21.

In one of its clauses, the treaty thus identified the contracting parties:

> Determined to sustain an energetic action in defense of the principles of representative democracy and of the traditional liberties of their peoples that are a living part of the Western world, which is also American and Christian.

In spite of this, as will be shown shortly, this instrument served Brazil in dragging Argentina toward its policy of protecting Castro, and toward its tendency to Oriental neutralism. The most important articles are the first two:

> Article 1: The High Contracting Parties, for the purpose of consolidating the links of friendship which unite them, agree to carry out permanent consultations on all matters of

common interest and to coordinate their activities in the continental and worldwide scope.

Article 2: For the same purpose, the High Contracting Parties agree to maintain an interchange of information on all the questions of relevant character in the international sphere.

Other articles referred to the strengthening of the inter-American system; to the consolidation of relations between Argentina and Brazil in the juridical, economic, financial, and cultural spheres; to the free transit of the nationals of both states; to the promotion of the necessary legislative dispositions; and, finally, to the circumstances that the treaty would stand open to the adherence of all the countries of the hemisphere.

Months later Deputy Camet revealed in Congress that "one of those who fought most enthusiastically to bring about the agreement with the Argentine Republic and who felt a great satisfaction when this agreement was signed" was the procommunist brother-in-law of Goulart, Lionel Brizzola, then governor of the state of Rio Grande do Sul. The later trajectory of Brizzola throws more precise lights on the sense of the Convention of Uruguayana.

Our foreign policy was closely linked to that of Brazil in the very moment when the latter was moving in an evident neutralist direction. Quadros was already making public the then imprudent attitudes of rapprochement to the communist world, which resulted in his losing the presidency. Thus, he promised emissaries to the meeting of the "neutrals" (which, with a marked anti-Western bias, was to take place in Belgrade), and in fact had sent them to Moscow and to Peking. The abuse of these gestures led to his curious abdication of August 25, 1961, which should have served as a warning signal to Frondizi's government.

The latter, five days before the resignation of Quadros, pre-

sented the Convention of Uruguayana to the Senate for ratification. In the solemn message of transmittal, the "exceptional
character" of the treaty was underscored. A citation of Pope John
XXIII came just before the materialist formula that said "For
it, our foreign policy is being placed consciously in the service
of development"—the echo of a phrase of the article which
Quadros wrote shortly before his fall saying "In time, the foreign policy of Brazil will reflect the craving for developmental
progress."

The fierce crisis in the neighboring country over a succession
to Quadros and the alarming tendencies of the Brazilian international behavior would never lead the Argentine Senate to
ratify the Convention of Uruguayana. In spite of the comfortable government majority, this body, according to *La Prensa*
(September 24, 1961), showed itself reticent about the treaty.
Frondizi and his advisors then had to push through the constitutional restraints and resort to the questionable method of an
exchange of notes in order to put the convention into execution.
On November 24 these notes were exchanged, and on November 28 the form in which the practice of consultation and interchange of information would be carried out was published. This
was based on a memorandum of Brazilian Foreign Minister
Francisco C. de San Tiago Dantas. The memorandum detailed
a complex system of mixed commissions to be made up of diplomatic officials who would be obliged at various levels to hold
daily, weekly, monthly, and semi-annual meetings of consultation. The notes exchanged were signed by Foreign Minister
Cárcano and Ambassador Boulitreau Fragoso.

Nothing reasonable justifies so blind an adherence to the interests of the neighboring country from which we are separated
by language, ethnic composition, and political history, apart
from a secular rivalry for continental domination. And still less,
in these moments when Brazil was orienting herself toward the
neutralist Afro-Asian bloc, outside the Western orbit.

In the above mentioned article, Quadros described the "new policy" of his country as the emergence of a "new force" on the world scene. He did not conceal her condition of an underdeveloped nation, which for the most part of his country became a stage for "quasi-Asiatic dramas." Although tied to the Western bloc and to inter-American obligations, Brazil according to Quadros could not limit herself to these bases and give up the points she had in common with Latin America and with the recently emancipated peoples of Asia and Africa, because this would be to "repudiate ties and contacts offering great possibilities for the national realization." The common factor is the necessity of "forming a single front in the battle against underdevelopment and all forms of oppression." Facing this, the United States and the Western world must "show and prove that it is not only communist planning that promotes the prosperity of national economies." And after affirming that there could be no sharing of ideals between the rich, cultivated areas of North America and the famine zones of the Brazilian Northeast, he made plain his point of view as follows:

> Thinking of this sort irrevocably creates in us a sense of solidarity with those povery-stricken peoples who, on three continents, are struggling against imperialist interests, which under the umbrella of democratic institutions mislead—if not destroy—attempts to organize popular economies.

Cuba revealed the nature of the continental crisis, and the reaction of Quadros was reduced to defending "with intransigence the sovereignty" of the island whose drama helped to "awaken the continent to a true awareness of its responsibilities." Regarding Africa, this represents today a "new dimension in Brazilian policy," and Brazil must claim links with the black continent in "cultural and ethnic roots and share its desire of forging an independent position in the world of today." In this manner it would be turned into the "bridge" between the West and the Afro-Asian bloc, an ideal that would not exclude economic advantages for the intermediary.

Quadros expressed also that Brazil was not a member of any bloc (which contradicts an earlier affirmation), does not want to participate in the cold war, and has not signed treaties of the nature of NATO (he forgot that the Rio treaty of 1947 was its antecedent); and he desired to maintain relations with all the world, including the communist. Finally, in concluding, he reiterated the scheme cited above: in Brazil, foreign policy has been converted into an instrument for a policy of development.

To this policy the Argentine government would adhere unconditionally by means of the Convention of Uruguayana. Not even author's rights would belong to our country, but only to the theoreticians of Itamaratí. The measure of this intellectual dependence is shown in the book of Hélio Jaguaribe, O Nacionalismo na atualidade brasilera, published officially in Brazil in the same year as Frondizi assumed the presidency of the Republic.

What was called the "spirit of Uruguayana" is prefigured in the work of this acute thinker, a Marxist nationalist, although of a heterodox Marxism which has incurred for him criticism from the communists. For Jaguaribe, Brazil is to claim in the sphere of international relations a "position of greater autonomy with regard to the United States and the great European powers inclining, at the same time, toward a neutralist line in regard to the North American-Soviet conflict." This is because the neutralist countries, situated between both blocs, command a power of negotiation over each bloc in accordance with their stratetgic importance. The book rejects—as was demonstrated by Frondizi—the notion of the West: "In our time there are not two cultures in conflict; there is only one culture—the Occidental-Universal civilization."

But the emancipation of Brazil from its dependence on North America requires an indispensable condition in order to "neutralize the power of reprisal in the United States": the union of

Latin America "based on a close, working relation between Brazil and Argentina." Jaguaribe envisions the "extraordinary power of negotiation that the Latin American countries might dispose in facing the United States." The disarticulation of these countries results essentially in the Brazilian-Argentine discord. Thus, as the close cooperation between both nations "could impose the general neutrality of the area on the United States," it would be "impossible for our neutralism, or at least much more difficult, if it were adopted in isolation to find, on the part of Argentina, a policy of hostility or lack of cooperation."

Frondizi and his team took pains to comply exactly with this policy set by a foreign chancery. The new minister of foreign relations, Adolfo Mugica, could exclaim from Rio on the eve of the Economic Meeting of Punta del Este: "We shall act without discrepancies or divergencies of any kind. We shall act as a single country. Argentina will make hers the proposals of Brazil and vice versa."

THE FINAL ERRORS

The above enthusiastic words were pronounced by Frondizi's third foreign minister, Adolfo Mugica, who had replaced Taboada shortly after the meeting in Uruguayana. The direction of foreign policy remained then publicly entrusted to a figure of former Conservative affiliation. Beside him as undersecretary of foreign relations was the former minister in Rio, Oscar H. Camilión. This appointment as well as other equally eloquent signs proved that nothing new would affect the orientation assumed by the Argentine government in the international sphere.

A Clandestine Visit

On August 18, 1961, at 10:20 A.M., the aerial taxi CX-AKP "Bonanza," proceeding from Uruguay, landed at the civil airport of Don Torcuato. Aboard was the Cuban minister of industry, Ernesto Guevara Lynch. The visitor was promptly led by personnel of the Presidential Guard to the presidential residence in Olivos, from which he departed about an hour later so as to be able to keep another appointment before his return flight to Uruguay at 2:17 that afternoon.

This visit, which would fundamentally upset the stability of Frondizi, was prepared with the greatest secrecy. Even though this news was kept from the military secretaries, it quickly came to the knowledge of the armed forces—giving rise to numerous meetings of commands, to the partial withdrawal of troops from the capital, and to diffusing radiograms to units in the interior. The distrust aroused by the "spirit of Uruguayana" created a crisis at the earliest opportunity, in the face of the tortuous procedures of the government.

Official explanations abounded without having cleared the confusion provoked by the abnormal arrangement of the Frondizi-Guevara interview. There were two communiqués from the Presidency, one August 18 and the other August 19; a message from Frondizi to the country August 21; and all this without taking into account the picturesque declarations of Foreign Minister Mugica which hastened his resignation. The President assumed personally all responsibility, although he never clarified why the visit had to be concealed, even from the Military Cabinet. He adduced vague motives of security, and avoiding the concrete incident he returned to his habitual digressions on development, to the diminishing concept of the West, and to the idea that, thanks to this same development, Argentina would convert herself within less than ten years into a "world power."

Dr. Mugica was not so discreet. He said that Guevara had requested a visa in order to have an interview with Frondizi, a version later denied by Guevara in Havana. But he added that the meeting had been planned in Punta del Este in a meeting between Castro's minister and Richard Goodwin, assistant to

President Kennedy, for the purpose of utilizing the mediation of the Argentine government between Cuba and the United States. The following day this version was in turn denied by Goodwin and the Department of State.

From this singular episode it may be deduced that for the second time the government tried to play "arbiter" between Washington and Havana without any success, for it only achieved the repudiation of both parties. However, in differentiation from the offer of good offices, Guevara's clandestine visit cracked the tenuous basis on which Frondizi was supporting himself, and it was the first clear symptom of his downfall. General Aramburu publicly withdrew his support of the government and in a declaration praised the military reactions to the episode.

On his part Guevara, after talking with the Argentine President, went to Brazil and there was cordially received, as well as decorated by Janio Quadros with the grand cross of the Cruzeiro do Sul. This reception ignited the grave constitutional crisis in Brazil, which was to extend itself from the resignation of Quadros to the conditional assumption of power by Goulart.

In our country Frondizi had to replace Mugica by a more predictable Conservative, Miguel Angel Cárcano, who hastened to declare on his arrival from Paris: "I come to serve the country and the policy of its President." His second promise was being literally fulfilled, perhaps to the impairment of the first and to the personal prestige of the new foreign minister. Immediately Undersecretary Camilión was confirmed, while Ambassador Musich was ostensibly withdrawn from San Martín Palace. He continued, however, to use his diplomatic title until another crisis, even more dynamic, would jolt the government.

Mendicancy and "Documents"

In the early part of September 1961, Presidents Alessandri and Frondizi met in Chile and produced the "Declaration of

Viña del Mar," in the text of which pro-Western affirmations and those favorable to representative democracy are eclectically compensated for with allusions to "peaceful coexistence" to nonintervention and to self-determination of peoples.

Late that month the Argentine chief of state went again to the United States to speak before the Assembly of the United Nations. In his speech he saluted the "greatest and most decisive event of our century that will give the historic name to our epoch . . . I refer to the heroic and great awakening of the new nationalities of Asia and Africa." The President not only gave praise but also offered the total Argentine solidarity:

> The Argentines greet with emotion their Asian and African brothers, and they promise their most decisive and fraternal collaboration in the arduous but rewarding process of securing their liberty and their growing prosperity—both for the peoples who have already achieved their political independence and those who are still fighting to obtain it.

Once more the word "West" aroused semantic concern in Frondizi, who again separated it from any antagonistic idea of a bloc. The interplanetary trips not only led him to laud the "miraculous emergence of the intelligence," but also moved him to further reflections:

> Nevertheless, on the earth in which this miracle is produced, two-thirds of its inhabitants live in poverty and lack of culture, while the nations accumulate weapons of destruction which, they know, are never to be brandished and which consume fabulous sums.
>
> I belong to a country which is a part of this backward portion of humanity. My people are realizing in this moment a tremendous sacrifice to overcome their crisis and to consolidate a political, democratic and economically independent community which will be prosperous and happy.

Fraternity with Asia and Africa led Frondizi to place his country in the "backward portion of humanity" among the two-thirds of mankind that "live in poverty and lack of culture."

The day before his entrance into international mendicancy, the President had a long interview with Kennedy. Its length was later exploited by official propaganda as a sign of North American sympathy, but the truth is that during the meeting copies of Cuban documents casting shadows on the international conduct of Argentina were delivered to Foreign Minister Cárcano. On October 1 the "Cuban documents" were divulged in the local press and the government ordered an investigation from which it deduced that it was a question of falsification, later attributed to Cuban exiles in Buenos Aires, but without a definitive clarification of the fact. The most paradoxical was the verisimilitude of the content of said "documents"—later to appear as the continual adjustment of Argentine foreign policy, in accordance with Wilde's axiom that nature imitates art.

The scandal made it impossible for the government to continue postponing the interpellation of the foreign minister, which for some time now the opposition blocs in the Chamber of Deputies had been soliciting without result. Finally Cárcano presented himself in the Chamber on October 27 to read a defense of the official diplomatic line. The interpellation could not be continued later on the new date that had been fixed by the Parliamentary maneuvers of the majority, and Cárcano then had to reply—with greater comfort for himself—in writing. The first exposition is sufficient to identify his idea of Argentine foreign policy.

The Argentine international policy has not been invented by the government: it has a historic continuity because it rests on traditional lines and is the expression of principles defined and defended by many illustrious men who gave prestige to the country in the continent and in the community of nations.

Was the Chancellor seeking to associate himself with these men by way of his wandering concept of hemispheric obligations?

This American system is still in elaboration and possesses the fragility of all new constructions. It is necessary to treat it with care and prudence and not to submit it to proofs of force or to political tensions that could weaken it while it is yet to be consolidated with tradition and great experience.

The youth of the system is relative, because the Lend-Lease regime served as antecedent to the Marshall Plan and the treaty of Rio to NATO. Besides, the best method to endow a juridical system with tradition and experience does not consist of violating its most explicit and urgent norms.

Argentina Protects Cuba

The ever firmer alliance of the Cuban government with Communist China and the Soviet Union (Soviet-Cuban communiqué of September 20, 1961, and Chinese-Cuban communiqué of October 2, 1961), and above all its attempts to "export the revolution" to other American countries through subversive maneuvers, obliged the OAS to again confront the problem. On October 25, 1961, the Council of the organization failed to take up a Peruvian motion to resort to collective action regarding Cuba, but toward the middle of the following month it approved a Colombian project on communist infiltration in America according to which, on December 4, it was decided to hold a consultation meeting of foreign ministers. In spite of some dilatory tactics, already in evidence, a majority of nineteen votes in favor was achieved with two against.

The Colombian plan sought to give Castro time to break his links with international communism. On the other hand, the dictator could not have found a more opportune moment to make public his sensational profession of faith as a communist.

"I am a Marxist-Leninist, and I will be until the end of my life," he unexpectedly confessed in the *Universidad Popular del Aire de La Habana* during one of his extensive televised talks.

The impression left by these words hardly disappeared when the Council of the OAS had to vote on the Colombian project. Now the last vestige of hope for the rectification of the Cuban regime had been destroyed by Castro himself. At least the decision for the delegates of the American nations was suddenly simplified: the necessity of a meeting of consultation now appeared clearer and more urgent than before.

At the moment the trend of the voting was not too clear. Opinions favoring the project on this occasion did not exceed fourteen. Mexico and Cuba voted against, and there were five abstentions: Argentina, Bolivia, Brazil, Chile, and Ecuador. The convocation of the meeting was agreed then by a comfortable majority; but the number of abstentions was a cause for concern, because the measure was perfectly justified by the gravity of the case and its form was in accordance with the terms of the Inter-American Treaty of Reciprocal Assistance.

In these debates, in anticipation of the Eighth Meeting of Consultation, the Argentine attitude was confused and dilatory. On October 25 our delegate had voted affirmatively, but according to a United Press dispatch (*La Prensa*, November 15, 1961), Argentina, together with Brazil, Chile, and Ecuador, had then tried in vain to defer the decision.

The Argentine abstention December 4 had a more explicit base. On the same day a communiqué from the Foreign Ministry released instructions to the ambassador at the OAS, Enrique E. Rivarola. The principal argument was the desire to preserve American unity, disregarding the project of Colombia, which was not shared by other countries. The truth is that our government did not want to base the meeting of consultation on Article 6 of the Rio Treaty—as did the Colombian proposal containing concrete measures applicable against Cuba—but rather on a more innocuous norm, that of Article 39 of the Charter of the OAS. The pretext of not dividing continental opinion served our government to shield Castro in fact. With these preliminaries, the forecasts about Argentine conduct in the forthcoming meeting of consultation (January 1962) at Punta del Este were logically pessimistic.

Toward the East

In the interval Frondizi undertook his final trip abroad, this time through Canada, Greece, and Asia. An important stage of the trip was in India where he held extensive discussions with the leaders of that country. With Nehru he talked for a total of more than seven hours. Each day it became more evident that the motive of the Asiatic trip was to reinforce the neutralist tendency of the Argentine government, which is obvious enough from Frondizi's speech at Delhi:

> These two great communities of the underdeveloped world, Latin America and India, are the two most important of the noncommunist political sector. The coordination of their policies on a world scale for the purpose of favoring their development can be a vital factor in the battle which the underdeveloped countries are undertaking.

Enthusiasm for the forging of new links with remote countries was not free of the poetic approach:

> I am aware that there exist profound differences in the philosophic concepts of the world between a nation of the East and another of the West. But I share the universal vision of Tagore when he says in one of his poems that *"Orient and Occident are no more than alternate beats of one single heart."*

In Bangkok December 9 Frondizi visited the headquarters of SEATO and improvised a pacifist harrangue hardly appropriate in an organization of military defense. A newspaperman recalls the episode as follows:

The kind of underlying neutralism that was contained in the words of the Argentine President, whose origin can probably be found in the long interviews with Prime Minister Nehru, caused great surprise, not only to the members of SEATO, but also to certain persons in the entourage of the President.

When the North American delegate proposed a vote of approval for Frondizi's words no one offered a second, and the embarrassing session had to be adjourned immediately.

Shortly afterward, now in Hong Kong, Frondizi declared to a gentleman of the press that the two Chinas would have to be represented in the United Nations. This opinion, favorable to the Peking regime, was formulated three days before the General Assembly rejected its entrance into the international organization by a strong majority.

The trip culminated with a visit to Kennedy. Frondizi advanced information from Honolulu that the North American President had invited him, but according to a cable in *La Nación*, Pierre Salinger, press chief of the White House, had to clarify that the initiative had come from Frondizi himself.

Denouement in Punta del Este

In the meantime, the date of the consultation meeting was approaching. Symptoms of the Argentine attitude revealed no improvement. On December 27 Cárcano received Cuban Vice Chancellor Carlos Olivares Sánchez, and in the official communiqué (later called "trascendido") the phrase on nonintervention and self-determination was not lacking. The same concept was ratified by Frondizi in his end-of-the-year message:

. . . the guiding principles of the Argentine presence in the

order of international relations, which are those of the invio-
lability of States and respect for self-determination of peoples,
have constituted our polestar and distinguished all our activities . . . the difficulties, the lack of comprehension, and the
opposition which we find on both fronts, the domestic and
the international, can only make us reaffirm our decision to
maintain our fixed directions.

On January 5, 1962, Frondizi flew to Montevideo for a meeting with Haedo. He declared to the newspapermen who asked
him about the forthcoming conference at Punta del Este:

Argentina maintains the principle of nonintervention and
of self-determination of peoples. It will abide by its adherence
to the Western and Christian philosophy proclaimed in
Uruguayana.

The declaration revealed the intimate sense of the convention
signed with Quadros, beyond that of the adjectives "Western
and Christian." The following day, like an echo in harmony, it
was Brazilian Foreign Minister Dantas who took the liberty of
denying the possibility of a change in the international position
of Argentina.

On January 7 it was reported from Washington that our country had presented through Ambassador del Carril a proposal to
achieve American unanimity in a resolution that would contain
no sanctions against Cuba. With the same goal in mind, a week
later, Undersecretary Camilión and Ambassador Ortiz de Rozas
traveled to the United States and Brazil. The same day, however,
Kennedy announced that sanctions would be applied to Cuba,
an opinion which was shortly repeated by Secretary of State
Rusk.

Cuba designated President Dorticós as her representative in
the Meeting of Consultation, a strange gesture without precedent that reduced a chief of state to the rank of foreign minister.
Passing through Brazil on the way to Punta del Este, Dorticós

had a long conversation with Goulart, from which he emerged satisfied with the attitude of that country regarding Cuba, "in defense of the principles of nonintervention and self-determination.

In addition to Foreign Minister Cárcano, the Argentine delegation comprised the following: Ambassadors Emilio Donato del Carril and Enrique Rivarola, Undersecretary Camilión, José María Alvarez de Toledo, Carlos Ortiz de Rozas, José María Ruda, Eduardo T. Pardo, Hugo Gobbi, César M. Gondra, Eduardo E. Clores, Gastón de Prat Gay, and Gustavo Figueroa. The Congress was represented by Senator Benjamín Guzmán and Deputy Angel Ramella.

The first sessions of the conference showed that the United States and Argentina were in agreement on the exclusion of Cuba, a measure against which there were only four adverse votes. This initial coincidence displeased Brazil. But on January 24 the Brazilian displeasure was transferred to the United States, because Argentina signed along with Bolivia, Brazil, Chile, Ecuador, Haiti, and Mexico a memorandum pointing out the necessity of a previous inter-American conference to reform the OAS charter, in order to be able to suspend or expel a communist member.

On the following day a speech from Cárcano summed up the contradictions of the Argentine delegation:

> Argentina does not desire, or is it proposed, to intervene in the internal affairs of Cuba. The Government of Cuba has raised in America the first flag of a regime which we resist and before which Argentina has defended her position categorically. It is no longer the suspicion of the early days, or the errors attributed to premature enthusiasm, or the necessity of defense of its Revolutionary Government, or the gratuitous accusation of damaged interests; now it is the explicit confession clamoring before the world its new profession of political faith so foreign to that of America: Marxism-Leninism. We

can and we must point out this fact, recognize it with sorrow but with frankness here in the OAS.

We defend and we shall continue defending the right of each country to make its own government. Each one is the master in seeking its destiny as it best interprets it or as its people desire, to live a life in the manner that it pleases.

But, in the face of this fact, the Argentine government tediously insisted on the principles of nonintervention and self-determination and made it clear that America must accept the challenge, which meant reckoning with a member of the community already linked to communism.

On January 27 Argentina appeared to favor the exclusion of Cuba from the inter-American system, although not the immediate exclusion the majority demanded, but by referring the case to the OAS for solution. Two days later, the adherence of the vacillating Haiti to the bloc favoring sanctions guaranteed to this sector a two-thirds majority, but the United States would have preferred to count on the vote of Argentina and Chile. Finally, on January 30, the conference approved the immediate exclusion of Cuba by fourteen votes in favor, one against (the Cuban), and six abstentions (Argentina, Bolivia, Brazil, Chile, Ecuador, and Mexico). This resolution, the sixth of the meeting of consultation, declared in its dispositive part:

1. That adherence by any member of the Organization of American States to Marxism-Leninism is incompatible with the inter-American system and the alignment of such a government with the communist bloc breaks the unity and solidarity of the hemisphere.

2. That the present Government of Cuba, which has officially identified itself as a Marxist-Leninist government, is incompatible with the principles and objectives of the inter-American system.

3. That this incompatibility excludes the present Government of Cuba from participation in the inter-American system.

4. That the Council of the Organization of American States and the other organs and organizations of the inter-American system adopt without delay the measures necessary to carry out this resolution.

As appears from the text, the conference resorted to the word "exclusion" instead of "expulsion."

Also there was approval of eight other documents, among which the most important referred to the maintenance of free elections, to the principles of nonintervention and self-determination of peoples (with the adverse vote of Cuba that could not repudiate the Sino-Soviet intervention in its internal policy), to the communist offensive in Latin America, to the immediate exclusion of Cuba from the Inter-American Defense Board, to the immediate cessation of trade in arms with Cuba and the possibility of extending the cessation to other strategic articles, as well as to the vigilance on the part of the OAS Council of the subversive acts from the Sino-Soviet bloc.

According to Cárcano, the Argentine abstention on Resolution VI (exclusion of Cuba from the OAS) was based on the following:

> Resuming then, from the juridical point of view, we understand that the Resolution departs from two basic principles of the norms of this regional organism; first, it concedes to the organ of consultation a faculty greater than that attributed by the Inter-American Treaty of Reciprocal Assistance and, second, it applies a norm that does not exist in the Charter of the OAS, for which the States that signed and ratified said instrument have not given their consent.
>
> Our country, I repeat, respectful of the juridical norms as the first principle of its international life, cannot support with its vote this Resolution which goes much further beyond the faculties to which it has given its consent.

On the same day, January 30, Frondizi had engaged in a

long telephone conversation with Goulart, after which he sent Julio López Muñiz with a sealed envelope to the Argentine foreign minister, prescribing the final abstention. The earlier instructions had already ordered abstention from all sanctions against Cuba, even though they might have been provided in the Rio Treaty of Assistance. After having hobbled as far as possible the meeting of the foreign ministers and after opposing sanctions explicitly provided in the treaty, the Argentine government took refuge in a questionable juridical argument—taken from domestic law—in order to continue protecting Castro.

The internal reaction to the abstention was sudden and uncontainable. On January 31 the military meetings multiplied, and the secretary of the air force gave General Order 29 to all his commands:

> The Argentine Air Force operating on the basis that the fight against communism is in accordance with a principle of defense more than of pure politics, and that international communism constitutes at present the greatest danger for liberty and democracy, reaffirms to the units its pro-Western position and its solidarity with all those countries that have taken up the defense of the free world, and it will not tolerate any threat that endangers our way of life.

It became evident that the armed forces were demanding of Frondizi rupture of diplomatic relations with Cuba, the replacement of Cárcano, and the dismissal of his collaborators. On February 1 the President and the military secretaries met in a three-hour session. On the following day there was another two-hour meeting, and an official communiqué was released from the office of the President, the text of which sought to explain the Argentine position:

> The Argentine Government will comply strictly and completely with all the Resolutions approved in Punta del Este. The position of abstention on the two indicated paragraphs

in no way diminishes the Argentine solidarity with those countries that voted for the Resolution.

Meanwhile, the military picture began to darken even more because Frondizi refused to fix a time for the rupture. On February 2 he summoned all the units of the three armed forces in the country. The rumor circulated that the military secretaries and the commanders in chief would resign, leaving the command in the hands of Frondizi in his character as commander in chief of the armed forces.

In spite of the intensity of the pressures, the President undertook a counterattack. On February 3 he traveled to Paraná for the purpose of inaugurating some new public works. But, surprisingly, he took advantage of the occasion to endorse the Argentine policy that had been followed at Punta del Este. In a violent speech he defended self-determination of peoples and maintained that the Argentine delegation to the meeting of consultation had not improvised, but had strictly followed, its instructions wherein it was affirmed:

> As I said to them verbally, and as I reiterate now in writing, we must be absolutely clear and precise. In spite of the cold war and the selfish interests that hide themselves behind it and in spite of the repeated attempts at penetration which international communism is making, it is fitting for us, the Argentines, to leave clearly established that what is being discussed in America is not the fate of an extremist caudillo who expresses himself in favor of a political order having nothing to do with the reality of our peoples, but the future of a group of underdeveloped nations that have decided freely to ascend through the higher levels of social and economic development. If this sovereign decision is not respected, if it is sought to hide or distort it in the ideological game of extremisms, then indeed the evil will be difficult to conjure away: an entire continent will be convulsed politically and socially.

In an intemperate tone, which recalled some of Perón's

addresses, he denounced the "frustrated politicians and resentful adventurers" whom "future generations will consign to fire," the "reactionary elements who are opposed to the liberations and development of our peoples because they prefer to maintain them in their colonial position," "certain Argentine organs of opinion," "certain newspapers," and "certain aggressive interests," as well as the never failing "monopolies" from North America.

The speech sought popular support with which to oppose the military pressure but evidently did not arouse the anticipated echo. On the contrary, the military tension continued to grow. On February 6, when the former king of Belgium, Leopold III, arrived at Buenos Aires, the military secretaries and the higher officials abstained from attending the dinner Frondizi arranged for the guest—at the last moment it was necessary to remove twenty-four places from the table. It became obvious that the treatment would be accorded to all official acts until there was a break with Cuba.

After this relatively restrained pace, events began to precipitate themselves. February 8 marked the return of the Argentine ambassador at Havana, Julio Amoedo, who was called by the Foreign Ministry. And on the same date the government broke diplomatic relations with Cuba and gave forty-eight hours to the Cuban representatives to leave the national territory. The following day it was announced that Switzerland would take charge of Argentine affairs in Havana, while Brazil would assume the same responsibility with respect to Cuban interests at Buenos Aires.

Once again, Frondizi gave way to pressures aroused by the gratuitous alternatives of the international policy, full of risks, which he had chosen. Nevertheless, his base of support was seriously affected. A new episode, this time in the domestic policy realm, would drag him from office a month later.

INTERNAL CONTRADICTIONS

In spite of its ambitious formulation, foreign policy was sown with deep internal contradictions. The pretension to originality or, in any case, to improvement on the old Argentine tradition in this matter, proved in practice to be a dull echo—or a modest copy of concepts elaborated with greater vigor by Itamaratí. As evidenced throughout this book, Brazil, after having drawn rich benefits from her collaboration with the United States during the war, was now inventing new techniques to continue obtaining advantages. Argentina, again, arrived too late.

On the other hand, the efforts to show our country as a "great world power" contradicted the tactics of mendacity and blackmail to which the diplomacy of Frondizi resorted. From this strange combination emerged the hybrid ideal of the "great underdeveloped power."

Another discordance in the foreign policy of these years is found in the refusal to accept the division of the world into blocs—instead a contradictory stress on notions incompatible with the idea of One World, such as sovereignty, self-determination of peoples, and absolute nonintervention, exacerbated in form of a myth. Thus, the theoretical adherence to the work of the United Nations in fact ran up against a virulent nationalism. Other consequences of similar contradiction were, on the one hand, to refer to our "Western and Christian" affiliation with gestures appropriate to the neutralist bloc, and on the other, the disdain of the hemispheric community on the pretext of avoiding the dangers that threatened it.

In sum, the foreign policy did not signify for Frondizi an instrument of consolidation and prestige, but an irritating factor, which in retrospect compromised his stability.

BIBLIOGRAPHY

Chapter 1

1. The World Crisis, 1929

Baumont, Maurice. La faillite de la paix (1919–1939). Paris: Presses Universitaires de France, 1960, Vol. I.

Moreno Quintana, Lucio M. Política económica. Buenos Aires: Librería del Colegio, 1944, Vol. I.

Morrison, Samuel Elliot, and Commager, Henry Steele. The Growth of the American Republic, 4th ed. New York: Oxford University Press, 1950.

2. The Imperial Conference of Ottawa, 1932

Argentine Republic, Chamber of Deputies, Sessions Report, 1933, Vol. II.

Argentine Republic, Ministry of Agriculture, Conferencia Económica Imperial de Ottawa, Buenos Aires, 1932.

Argentine Republic, Senate, Sessions Report, 1933, Vol. I.

García-Pelayo, Manuel. "El Imperio Británico." Revista de Occidente (1945).

Moreno Quintana. Política económica, Vol. I.

Olariaga, Nemesio de. El ruralismo argentino (Economía ganadera). Buenos Aires: El Ateneo, 1943.

3. The Statism of the Conservatives

Argentine Republic, Executive Branch (1932–1938), Vol. I, Hacienda, Buenos Aires, 1938.

Justo, Agustín P. "Nueva política comercial" (speech in the Bolsa de Comercio, June 3, 1933). La Nación, June 4, 1933.

Moreno Quintana. Política económica, Vol. II.

Portnoy, Leopoldo. La realidad argentina en el siglo XX, Vol. II: Análisis crítico de la economía. Buenos Aires: Fondo de Cultura Económica, 1961.

Sánchez Sorondo, Matías G. El problema ganadero ante el Congreso, 1922–1923. Buenos Aires: 1933.

Sociedad Rural Argentina, El pool de frigoríficos Necesidad de la intervención del Estado, Buenos Aires, 1927.

4. The Roca-Runciman Convention

Argentine Republic, Chamber of Deputies, *Sessions Record*, 1933, Vol. II.

Argentine Republic, Executive Branch (1932–1938), Vol. VIII, *Relaciones Exteriores y Culto*, Buenos Aires, 1938.

Argentine Republic, Ministry of Foreign Relations Archives, Commercial Division, England, 1932, dossier 152, *Convenio con Gran Bretaña, Iniciación de gestiones tendientes a celebrar un convenio con Gran Bretaña*, file II.

Argentine Republic, Senate, *Sessions Record*, 1933, Vol. I.

Bemis, Samuel Flagg. *The Latin American Policy of the United States.* New York: Harcourt Brace, 1943.

Moreno Quintana. *Política económica*, Vol. I.

Olariaga. *El ruralismo argentino.*

Pendle, George. *Argentina*, 3rd ed. New York: Oxford University Press, 1963.

Pereda, H. V. "Cómo se han cumplido en 1933 el Convenio Roca y los tratados de Ottowa." *La Nación*, April 29, 1934.

Universidad de Buenos Aires, Facultad de Derecho, *Antecedentes parlamentarios de la legislación argentina, I: Comercio de carnes (1862–1941)*, Buenos Aires, 1942.

5. *Parliamentary Debate*

Argentine Republic, Chamber of Deputies, *Sessions Report*, 1933, Vol. II.

Argentine Republic, Senate, *Sessions Report*, 1933, Vol. I.

6. *A Precedent*

Argentine Republic, Senate, *Sessions Report*, 1949, Vol. II, pp. 1437–1466.

Del Mazo, Gabriel. *El radicalismo. Notas sobre su historia y doctrina (1922–1952).* Buenos Aires: Raigal, 1955.

Moreno Quintana. *Política económica*, Vol. I.

7. *Ideological Echoes, the Theme of Imperialism*

Cafiero, Antonio R. *Cinco años después.* Buenos Aires: 1961.

"El fantasma imperialista." *El Príncipe*, 4 (May 1961), 35.

Guillén, Abraham. *La conspiración de la oligarquía (Radiografía del Plan Prebisch).* Buenos Aires: Guitem, 1956.

Irazusta, Rodolfo, and Irazusta, Julio. *La Argentina y el imperialismo británico.* Buenos Aires: Tor, 1934.

Jauretche, Arturo. *F.O.R.J.A. y la década infame.* Buenos Aires: Coyoacán, 1962.

Liceaga, José V. *Las carnes en la economía argentina.* Buenos Aires: Raigal, 1952.

Lozano, Jorge M. "Libros que hicieron la Argentina: Política británica en el Río de la Plata." *El Príncipe*, 9 (March 1962), 21.

Ortiz, Ricardo M. *Historia de la economía argentina*. Buenos Aires: Raigal, 1955.

Puiggrós, Rodolfo. *Libre empresa o nacionalización en la industria de la carne*. Buenos Aires: Argumentos, 1957.

Scalabrini Ortiz, Raúl. *Política británica en el Río de la Plata*. Buenos Aires: Reconquista, no date.

Chapter 2

Argentine Republic, Inter-American Conference for the Maintenance of Peace, *Sessions Report* (stenographic record in Spanish), Buenos Aires, 1937.

Argentine Republic, Ministry of Foreign Relations, *La política argentina en la Guerra del Chaco*, Buenos Aires, 1937.

Bemis, Samuel Flagg. *The Latin American Policy of the United States*. New York: Harcourt Brace, 1943.

Caicedo Castilla, José J. *El panamericanismo*. Buenos Aires: Depalma, 1961.

Drago, Mariano J. "Nuestra política exterior." *La Nación*, extra edition of May 22, 1960.

Duggan, Laurence. *The Americas: The Search for Hemispheric Security*. New York: 1949.

Hull, Cordell. *The Memoirs of Cordell Hull*. New York: Macmillan, 1948.

International Conferences of American States (1889–1936). Washington: Carnegie Endowment for International Peace, 1938.

McGann, Thomas F. *Argentina, the United States and the Inter-American System 1880–1914.*

Perkins, Dexter. *A History of the Monroe Doctrine*. Boston: Little, Brown, 1963.

Peterson, Harold F. *Argentina and the United States*. Albany: State University of New York, 1964.

Saavedra Lamas, Carlos. *Por la paz de las Américas*. Buenos Aires: Gleizer, 1937.

Silva, Carlos A. *La política internacional de la Nación Argentina*. Buenos Aires: Ministerio del Interior, Subsecretaría de Informaciones, 1946.

Smith, O. Edmund, Jr. *Yankee Diplomacy, United States Intervention in Argentina*. Dallas: Southern Methodist University Press, 1953.

Welles, Sumner. *Time for Decision*. New York: Harper, 1944.

Whitaker, Arthur P. *The United States and Argentina*. Cambridge: Harvard University Press, 1954.

————. "The Inter-American System," *Inter-American Affairs, 1942*. New York: Columbia University Press, 1943.

Chapter 3

1. *The First Steps*

Argentine Republic, Ministry of Foreign Relations Archives, 1939, dossier 68, European War, *Contrabando de guerra. Disposiciones adoptadas por el gobierno inglés.*

Argentine Republic, Ministry of Foreign Relations Archives, 1939, dossier 91, European War, *Disposiciones adoptadas por el gobierno alemán para reprimir el contrabando de guerra. Enumeración de los artículos considerados como tales.*

Argentine Republic, Ministry of Foreign Relations Archives, 1939, dossier 85, European War, *Posición de la República Argentina y el Brasil frente a los problemas que plantea el conflicto armado europeo. Misión del contralmirante Guisasola.*

2. *Panama, 1939*

Bemis, Samuel Flagg. *The Latin American Policy of the United States.* New York: Harcourt Brace, 1943.

Peterson, Harold F. *Argentina and the United States, 1810–1960.* Albany: State University of New York, 1964.

Silva, Carlos A. *La política internacional de la Nación Argentina.* Buenos Aires: Ministerio del Interior, Subsecretaría de Informaciones, 1946.

Smith, O. Edmund, Jr. *Yankee Diplomacy, United States Intervention in Argentina.* Dallas: Southern Methodist University Press, 1953.

Welles, Sumner. *Time for Decision.* New York: Harper, 1944.

Whitaker, Arthur P. "The Inter-American System," *Inter-American Affairs, 1942.* New York: Columbia University Press, 1943.

3. *Revision of Neutrality*

Argentine Republic, Ministry of Foreign Relations Archives, 1940, dossier 185, Circular 2, December 5, 1940, from Foreign Minister Cantilo to the Argentine Legations and Embassies: Note 226, from Ambassador Espil to the Foreign Ministry, April 27, 1940.

Bagú, Sergio. *La realidad argentina en el siglo XX*, Vol. III, *Argentina en el mundo.* Buenos Aires: Fondo de Cultura Económica, 1961.

Cantilo, José María: "Evolución de la neutralidad." *La Prensa*, November 17, 1943.

4. *Havana, 1940*

Bemis. *The Latin American Policy of the United States.*

Hull, Cordell. *The Memoirs of Cordell Hull.* New York: Macmillan, 1948.

Peterson. *Argentina and the United States, 1810–1960.*

Silva. *La política internacional de la Nación Argentina.*

Smith. *Yankee Diplomacy, United States Intervention in Argentina.*

Spykman, Nicholas J. *America's Strategy in World Politics.* New York: Harcourt Brace, 1942.

Whitaker. "The Inter-American System."

5. *Economic Measures*

Campbell, John C. "Nationalism and Regionalism in South America."

Foreign Affairs, 21 (October 1942), 132–148.
Whitaker. "The Inter-American System."

6. After Pearl Harbor

Argentine Republic, Chamber of Deputies, Sessions Report, 1942, Vol. VI, pp. 46 ff.
Bemis. The Latin American Policy of the United States.
Foreign Relations of the United States, 1942, Vol. V, The American Republics. Washington: United States Government Printing Office, 1962.
Hull. Memoirs.
Lanús, Adolfo. Campo minado. Buenos Aires: 1942.
Peterson. Argentina and the United States, 1810–1960.
Pinedo, Federico. La Argentina en la vorágine. Buenos Aires: Editorial Mundo Forense, 1943.
Ruiz Guiñazú, Enrique. La política argentina y el destino de América. Buenos Aires: Editorial Huemel, 1944.
Smith. Yankee Diplomacy, United States Intervention in Argentina.
Toynbee, A. J., and Veronica, eds. The War and the Neutrals. New York: Oxford University Press, 1956.
Welles. Time for Decision.
————. Where Are We Heading? New York: Harper, 1946.

7. Contradictions of Neutralism

Argentine Republic, Chamber of Deputies, Sessions Report, 1942, Vol. VI, pp. 46 ff.
Ruiz, Guiñazú. La política argentina y el destino de América.

Chapter 4

1. The Spears and Christian Missions

Argentine Republic, Ministry of Foreign Relations Archives, 1940, dossier 192, Political Division, European War, Proyecto del gobierno de los Estados Unidos sobre defensa continental.
Foreign Relations of the United States, 1942, Vol. V, The American Republics. Washington: United States Government Printing Office, 1962.

2. The Lend-Lease Act

Argentine Republic, Ministry of Foreign Relations Archives, 1941, dossier 289, European War, Proyecto de ley presentado por el Presidente Roosevelt al Congreso.
Les Archives Secrètes de la Wilhelmstrasse, Vol. V, Book II. Paris: Plon, 1954.
Perroux, François. "El don: su significación económica en el capitalismo contemporáneo." Diógenes (June 1954).
Stettinius, Edward R., Jr. Le Prét-Bail: arme de victoire. Origine et de-

veloppement de la Loi de Prét-Location. New York: Transatlantique, 1944.

Whitaker, Arthur P. "The Inter-American System," *Inter-American Affairs, 1942.* New York: Columbia University Press, 1943.

3. *The Lapez-Sueyro Mission*

Argentine Republic, Ministry of Foreign Relations Archives, 1941, dossier 64, Armaments Division, *Sobre provisión de materiales destinados a nuestras fuerzas armadas por la industria norteamericana,* Vols. I and II.

Hull, Cordell. *The Memoirs of Cordell Hull.* New York: Macmillan, 1948.

Ruiz Guiñazú, Enrique. *La política argentina y el destino de América.* Buenos Aires: Editorial Huemel, 1943.

Welles, Sumner. *Time For Decision.* New York: Harper, 1944.

————. *Where Are We Heading?* New York: Harper, 1946.

4. *The Consequences*

Brazil at War. New York: Brazilian Government Trade Bureau, 1945.

"Documentos para la historia." *La Vanguardia,* July 17, 1945, and September 18, 1945.

Documents on American Foreign Relations, 1941–42, Vol. IV. Boston: World Peace Foundation, 1942.

Foreign Relations of the United States, 1942, Vol. V.

Holmes, Olive. "Brazil: Rising Power in the Americas." *Foreign Policy Reports,* October 15, 1945.

Nef, John U. *War and Human Progress.* Cambridge: Harvard University Press, 1950.

Ringwood, O.K.D., and Holmes, Olive. "Status of Brazilian-U.S. War Agreements." *Foreign Policy Reports,* October 15, 1945.

Toynbee, A. J. *Civilization on Trial.* New York: Oxford University Press, 1948.

————, and Veronica, eds. *The War and the Neutrals.* New York: Oxford University Press, 1956.

Twentieth Report to Congress on Lend-Lease Operations for the Period Ending June 30, 1945. Washington: United States Government Printing Office, 1945.

Chapter 5

1. *Recognition*

Greenup, Ruth and Leonard. *Revolution Before Breakfast, Argentina 1941–1946.* Chapel Hill: University of North Carolina Press, 1947.

Hull, Cordell. *The Memoirs of Cordell Hull.* New York: Macmillan, 1948.

Josephs, Ray. *Argentine Diary.* New York: Random House, 1944.

Kelly, David. *The Ruling Few, or the Human Background to Diplomacy.* London: Hollis and Carter, 1952.

Patrón Costas, R. *Discurso que debió pronunciar en la convención del Partido Demócrata Nacional con motivo de la proclamación de su candidatura a la Presidencia de la Nación, 1943.*

Peterson, Harold F. *Argentina and the United States, 1810–1960.* Albany: State University of New York, 1964.

Rennie, Ysabel Fisk. *The Argentine Republic.* New York: Macmillan, 1945.

Smith, O. Edmund, Jr. *Yankee Diplomacy, United States Intervention in Argentina.* Dallas: Southern Methodist University Press, 1953.

Weil, Felix J. *Argentine Riddle.* New York: John Day, 1944.

Welles, Sumner. *Where Are We Heading?* New York: Harper, 1946.

Whitaker, Arthur P. "The Inter-American System," *Inter-American Affairs, 1942.* New York: Columbia University, 1943.

2. *The Promised Rupture*

Hull. *Memoirs.*

Peterson. *Argentina and the United States, 1810–1960.*

Smith. *Yankee Diplomacy.*

3. *Storni's Letter*

Argentine Republic, Ministry of Foreign Relations Archives, 1941, dossier 64, Armaments Division, *Sobre provisión de materiales destinados a nuestras fuerzas armadas por la industria norteamericana.*

Argentine Republic, Ministry of Foreign Relations Archives, 1943, dossier 1, *Guerra entre los Estados Unidos y los países del Eje,* Vol. XIII.

Kelly. *The Ruling Few.*

Smith. *Yankee Diplomacy.*

4. *The Rupture*

Department of State, *Consultation among the American Republics with respect to the Argentine Situation,* Washington, 1946 (the "Blue Book").

Hull. *Memoirs.*

Smith. *Yankee Diplomacy.*

Welles, Sumner. Statement reported in the *Washington Post,* December 29, 1943.

Whitaker. "The Inter-American System."

5. *Hull's Wrath*

Hull. *Memoirs.*

Kelly. *The Ruling Few.*

Perón, Juan D. "Significado de la defensa nacional desde el punto de vista militar." *El pueblo quiere saber de qué se trata.* Buenos Aires: 1944.

Smith. *Yankee Diplomacy.*

Toynbee, A. J., and Veronica, eds. *The War and the Neutrals.* New York: Oxford University Press, 1956.

Welles. *Where Are We Heading?*

Whitaker. "The Inter-American System."
Woodward. Llewellyn. *British Foreign Policy in the Second World War.*
    London: Her Majesty's Stationery Office, 1962.
6. *Counteroffensive and Arrangement*
Hull. *Memoirs.*
Smith. *Yankee Diplomacy.*
Toynbee. *The War and the Neutrals.*
Welles. *Where Are We Heading?*
Whitaker. "The Inter-American System."
7. *The San Francisco Conference*
Peterson. *Argentina and the United States, 1810–1960.*
Smith. *Yankee Diplomacy.*
Toynbee. *The War and the Neutrals.*
Welles. *Where Are We Heading?*
Woodward. *British Foreign Policy in the Second World War.*
8. *Blue Book's Blues*
Argentine Republic, Ministry of Foreign Relations, *La República Argen-
    tina ante el "Libro Azul,"* Buenos Aires, 1946.
Department of State, *Consultation among the American Republics with
    Respect to the Argentine Situation.*
Halperín Donghi, Tulio. "Crónica del período." *Argentina, 1930–1960.*
    Buenos Aires: Editorial Sur, 1961.
Kelly. *The Ruling Few.*
Toynbee. *The War and the Neutrals.*
Welles. *Where Are We Heading?*

Chapter 6

1. *After February*
Bruce, James. *Those Perplexing Argentines.* New York: Longmans, Green
    & Co., 1953.
Peterson, Harold F. *Argentina and the United States, 1810–1960.* Albany:
    State University of New York, 1964.
Argentine Republic, Ministry of Foreign Relations, *Memoria del Minis-
    terio de Relaciones Exteriores y Culto, 1946–47,* Buenos Aires, 1947.
Smith, O. Edmund, Jr. *Yankee Diplomacy, United States Intervention in
    Argentina.* Dallas: Southern Methodist University Press, 1953.
Toynbee, A. J., and Veronica, eds. *The War and the Neutrals.* New York:
    Oxford University Press, 1956.
Whitaker, Arthur P. *The United States and Argentina.* Cambridge: Har-
    vard University Press, 1954.
2. *The Rio Treaty*
Argentine Republic, Ministry of Foreign Relations, *Memoria del Minis-*

terio de Relaciones Exteriores y Culto, 1947–48, Buenos Aires (no date).

Caicedo Castilla, José J. El panamericanismo. Buenos Aires: Depalma, 1961.

Corominas, Enrique V. Historia de las conferencias interamericanas. Buenos Aires: Editorial Cívicas Argentinas, 1959.

Peterson. Argentina and the United States, 1810–1960.

Smith. Yankee Diplomacy.

Whitaker. The United States and Argentina.

3. The Economic War

Argentine Republic, Academy of Economic Sciences, Fondo Monetario Internacional y Banco Internacional de Reconstrucción (Acuerdos de Bretton Woods), Buenos Aires, 1945.

Argentine Republic, Senate, Sessions Report, 1949, Vol. II, pp. 1426–1433. (Molinari's speeches at the Havana Conference, 1947 and 1948).

Cafiero, Antonio F. Cinco años Después, Buenos Aires: 1961.

Claude, Henri. Le Plan Marshall. Paris: Editions Sociales, 1948.

Cuba en la Conferencia sobre Comercio y Empleo. Carta de la Habana, Havana, Publications of the Ministry of State (no date).

"Descartes." Política y estrategia (No ataco, critico). Buenos Aires: 1951.

Frantz, Harry W. "Beneficios que podría lograr la Argentina del Plan Marshall." La Prensa, January 24, 1948.

Giovanelli, Jorge A. El Plan Marshall y la lucha de los Estados Unidos contra el communismo. Buenos Aires: Academia de Ciencias Económicas, 1957.

Lévy-Jacquemin, Jacques. Grandeur ou décadence du Plan Marshall. Le carrefour du demain. Paris: M. Riviére, 1948.

Lucchini, Rolando G. El Plan Marshall. La posición argentina. Buenos Aires: Editorial Periplo, 1961.

———. Estatización del capital, crisis y transformación. Capitalismo de Estado y Socialismo de Estado Plan Marshall. Buenos Aires: Editorial Verdades, 1955.

Peyret, Henri. Le Plan Marshall, peut-il sauver l'Europe? Paris: S.E.F.I., 1948.

Pinedo, Federico. "El desarrollo económico-financiero." La Nación, extra edition of May 22, 1960.

Portnoy, Leopoldo. "La realidad argentina en el siglo XX." Análisis crítico de la economía, Vol. II. Buenos Aires: Fondo de Cultura Económica, 1961.

United States Statutes at Large, Vol. 62, Part I, pp. 137 ff.

4. Perón and the British

Argentine Republic, Chamber of Deputies, Sessions Report, 1949, Vol. IV.

Argentine Republic, Ministry of Foreign Relations, *Memoria del Ministerio de Relaciones Exteriores y Culto, 1947–48.*

Cafiero. *Cinco años después.*

Irazusta, Julio. *Perón y la crisis argentina.* Buenos Aires: Editorial La Voz, 1956.

Messner, Johannes. *El experimento inglés del socialismo.* Madrid: Editorial Rialp, 1957.

Owen, Frank. *Perón, His Rise and Fall.* London: Crescent Press, 1957.

Pendle, George. *Argentina,* 3rd ed. New York: Oxford University Press, 1963.

Puiggrós, Rodolfo. *Libre empressa o nacionalización en la industria de la carne.* Buenos Aires: Argumento, 1957.

Toynbee, A. J., and Veronica, eds. *The Realignment of Europe.* New York: Oxford University Press, 1955.

5. *Perón and Pan-Americanism*

Argentine Republic, Ministry of Foreign Relations, *La República Argentina en la IX Conferencia Internacional Americana,* Buenos Aires, 1949.

Caidedo Castilla. *El panamericanismo.*

Peterson. *Argentina and the United States, 1810–1960.*

Smith. *Yankee Diplomacy.*

6. *The Korean Crisis*

Argentine Republic, Chamber of Deputies, *Sessions Report,* 1951, Vol. I, pp 681 ff.

Peterson. *Argentina and the United States, 1810–1960.*

Smith. *Yankee Diplomacy.*

Whitaker. *The United States and Argentina.*

7. *Economic Union*

Argentine Republic, Ministry of Foreign Relations, *Expresiones de una política continental: Argentina y Nicaragua bajo el signo de América,* Buenos Aires, 1953.

Argentine Republic, Ministry of Foreign Relations, *Expresiones de una política continental: Discursos de los presidentes Chaves y Perón,* Buenos Aires, 1953.

Argentine Republic, Ministry of Foreign Relations, *Mensaje a los pueblos de América de los presidentes Perón e Ibáñez,* Buenos Aires, 1953.

Argentine Republic, Ministry of Foreign Relations, *Unión Económica Argentino-Ecuatoriana: Afirmación de un destino común,* Buenos Aires, 1953.

Magnet, Alejandro. *Nuestros vecinos justicialistas.* Santiago de Chile: Editorial del Pacífico, 1953.

Pendle. *Argentina.*

9. *Perón and His Opponents*

Naya, Enrique. "La crisis argentina: peronismo y antiperonismo." *Cuader-*

nos, 43 (July-August 1960).

Peterson. *Argentina and the United States, 1810–1960.*

Chapter 7

Camilión, Oscar H. "Objectivos permantes de la política exterior de la Argentina" (lecture given in the Centro de Altos Estudios del Ejército). *Boletín de la Dirección General de Política,* 66 (March 30, 1961).

From *Criterio,* the following articles with corresponding numbers of issues:

"La mediación argentina," 1376.

"De la Antártida a Uruguayana," 1379.

"De Tito a Quadros," 1381.

"La política de Brasil y Argentina," 1384.

"Crisis en nuestra política exterior," 1387.

"El encuentro de Viña del Mar," 1388.

"La Argentina en las Naciones Unidas," 1389.

"Dos versiones de la política exterior," 1392.

"Confesión de Castro y abstención argentina," 1393–1394.

"Actualización de Uruguayana," 1393–1394.

"La Reunión de Punta del Este y sus consecuencias," 1397.

Cúneo, Dardo. *Las nuevas fronteras.* Buenos Aires: Editorial Transición, 1964.

Domenicis, Lauro. "Alianza para el Progreso." *El Príncipe,* 5 (July 1961, 440).

―――――. "Después de Punta del Este." *El Príncipe,* 6 (September 1961).

From *El Príncipe,* the following articles:

"Intervención, doctrina de América," 4 (May 1961).

"La política exterior," 4 (May 1961).

"La cancillería a la deriva," 6 (September 1961).

"De Kamchatka al Chocón," 7 (November 1961).

"Ocaso de una política," 9 (March 1962).

Finer, Samuel E. *The Man on Horseback. The Role of the Military in Politics.* London: Pall Mall Press, 1962.

Florit, Carlos A. *Política exterior nacional.* Buenos Aires: Editorial Arayú, 1961.

Frigerio, Rogelio. *Nacionalismo, potencias industriales y subdesarrollo.* Buenos Aires: Editorial Concordia, 1961.

Frondizi, Arturo. *Argentina y América Latina.* Buenos Aires: Presidencia de la Nación, 1958.

―――――. *Europa y el desarrollo argentino.* Buenos Aires: Presidencia de la Nación, 1960.

―――――. *Política exterior argentina.* Buenos Aires: Editorial Transición, 1962.

Jaguaribe, Hélio. *O nacionalismo na atualidade brasileira*. Rio de Janeiro: Ministério de Educaçáo e Cultura, Instituto de Estudos Brasileiros, 1958.

Naya, Enrique. "La crisis argentina: peronismo y antiperonismo." *Cuadernos*, 43 (July-August 1960), 45–54.

Oría, Jorge S. "Punta del Este y el desarrollo económico." *El Príncipe*, 8 (December 1961), 19–28.

Peterson, Harold F. *Argentina and the United States, 1810–1960*. Albany: State University of New York, 1964.

Quadros, Jánio. "Brazil's New Foreign Policy." *Foreign Affairs*, 40, (October 1961), 19–28.

INDEX OF NAMES

235

Alberto A. Conil Paz is a well-known lawyer in Buenos Aires, and Gustavo E. Ferrari is presently teaching in the department of political science at one of Argentina's foremost schools. Their assessment of policy and politics offers a critical appraisal of a controversial South American era from an Argentine viewpoint.

Professor Kennedy is the director of the Program of Latin American Studies at the University of Notre Dame. He received his B.A. degree from the University of New Mexico and his M.A. and Ph.D. degrees from Columbia University. He is a frequent contributor to political science journals and magazines and is the author of *Catholicism, Nationalism and Democracy in Argentina*.